Interrail Ramblings: An A-Z Travelogue

BRENDAN JAMES

Copyright © 2024 Brendan James

All rights reserved.

ISBN: 9798329799651

ACKNOWLEDGEMENTS

Massive thanks to Margaret for editing and to Lauren for the lovely cover; and to all my friends and family for their encouragement and support. Thank you also to loved ones and strangers who have travelled with me over the years, and not least of all, to those of you picking up this book.

For mom and dad

CONTENTS

Introduction	1
A1 Amsterdam to Paris	7
A2 Amsterdam to Milan	12
A3 Århus to Copenhagen	18
B1 Budapest to Bucharest	22
B2 Bergen to Voss	27
C1 Cologne to Geneva	32
C2 Cambridge to Amsterdam	36
D1 Duisburg to Innsbruck	41
D2 Dortmund to Liège	46
E1 Elsinore to Amsterdam	54
E2 Eskişehir to Istanbul	57
F1 Fredericia to Hamburg	65
F2 Freiburg to Basle	69
G1 Geneva to Venice	75
G2 Groningen to Leer	80
H1 Heidelberg to Ostend	86

INTERRAIL RAMBLINGS

H2 Hilversum to Bruges	91
I Istanbul to Bucharest	97
J Jesenice to Zagreb	105
K1 Krakow to Berlin	111
K2 Kehl to Strasbourg	116
L1 Lichfield to Antwerp	122
L2 London to Paris/Brussels	128
M1 Moscow to London	134
M2 Munich to Berchtesgaden and Salzburg	142
M3 Malaga to Cordoba	146
N1 Nice to Monte Carlo and Ventimiglia	154
N2 New York to Poughkeepsie	161
O Ostend to Warsaw	166
P1 Prague to Krakow	174
P2 Porto to Pinhão	178
Q Moscow to Vologda	183
R1 Ruse to Varna	189
R2 Riga to Sigulda	193

S1 Stockholm to Oslo	198
S2 Saint Petersburg to Veliky Novgorod	203
T1 Tunis to Sousse	210
T2 Trieste to Ljubljana	214
U1 Utrecht to the Hook of Holland	221
V1 Vienna to Gdansk	233
V2 Vienna to Bratislava	238
W Wolverhampton to Lyon	245
X for eXotic: Metlaoui to Redeyef	253
Y for 'whY didn't I ever …'	257
Z1 Zürich to Villach	266
Z2 Zakopane to Krakow	271

Introduction

Like a lot of people, I've always loved travelling abroad on trains. And this book is all about doing that, largely in Europe but now and again elsewhere too. It chronicles some of the more memorable journeys I've been on and also touches on the history of some of the trains and routes involved. In the process, there's a bit about me too – not in a full-on memoir kind of way but slightly more peripherally. After all, it was *me* doing these journeys at different points in *my* life - quite a few of them on my own, some with Margaret, my ex-wife and lifelong friend and some with David, my husband (yes, that's an altogether different book).

Trains are actually very close to my heart for a number of reasons, the main one being that foreign rail travel opened up my world as a teenager and changed me as a person. It allowed me to venture beyond the narrow confines of where I grew up and took me to places where I made new friends. It gave me the opportunity to experience the thrill of using languages I was learning at school (and later university). It also created a sense that life was full of potential. Armistead Maupin, the American novelist, writes somewhat despondently about travel; he said it "might be broadening for a while, but sooner or later, it just narrowed your illusions about who you could be." That may well be true in later life - and as I approach sixty, I can certainly relate more to what he means. But in my younger years, overseas train travel always made me believe there were endless possibilities – of new people to meet, new places to see, new ways to live and be. It might just have been that special feeling you get from being abroad, described so beautifully by Hannah Arendt: "Loving life is easy when you are abroad. Where no one knows you and you hold your life in your hands all alone, you are more a master of yourself than at any other time." And because it was trains that took me abroad, one way or another they also became bound up in that wonderful feeling.

Some of these possibilities transpired for me in genuinely life-changing ways – work experience in Germany and France, living and studying in Holland, youthful romance in Denmark, for instance. At other times, train journeys were just fun ways of getting from A to B but that didn't matter – for me, there was always that rich sense of potential that ended up imbuing train travel with excitement and positivity. There's something else too - when you're on a train journey, life suddenly seems to have a very clear purpose; getting from A to B becomes the be-all and end-all for the duration of that journey – you know exactly where you're going, and getting there is your entire purpose and mission; even though you're just sitting on your backside, every minute is one well spent and getting you closer to achieving your aim.

For all these reasons, I developed quite a fascination with trains and with travelling on them. This fascination also ended up being responsible for a railway hobby I've had for nigh on forty years now - collecting train destination signs (which show the train's name, destination and calling-points). Whichever town or city I've been to since I started collecting, I've called in at the relevant station office or depot to ask if they have any spare or disused ones. And though reactions have varied from bemused to amused and even downright dismissive, my enquiries have often been richly rewarded. And a letter I once sent to PKP (Polish Railways) in the 1980s even led to a lifelong friendship with Marek, the person who happened to open the envelope in Warsaw (more on him later).

In the chapters that follow, I've put together a personal A-Z of some of my most memorable train journeys, each letter representing the various departure points (and as you'll see, most letters have two or three entries). The A to Z structure seemed as good a way as any to organise this collection of lifetime travel memories. The journeys were memorable for all sorts of reasons – because they were particularly scenic, challenging and/or enjoyable; because of the people I met on them, or because of what led up to them or happened afterwards. And to reconstruct them here, I've drawn on old diaries, tickets, notebooks, and most unreliably of all, my own memory.

Structuring these mini-travelogues in this A-Z way means the sections aren't of course in chronological order – some of the journeys were made when I was still a teenager, others in my thirties and some much more recently. But that doesn't really matter; the focus is on the trips and the trains themselves, particularly in the case of renowned international services like the Orient Express, the Northern Arrow or the Tauern Express and so on. And though this is in no way intended as a travel guide (let's face it, there are plenty of them already) I inevitably touch on my impressions of most of the towns and cities visited.

I should also say that even though I've called the book *Interrail Ramblings*, not *all* the journeys here were actually done on Interrail trips. That said, a good many of them were – my first Interrail trip was under the pre-26 scheme, the three or four other times were 26+. But as train trips overseas, they are all ***inter*national *rail*** journeys. Some of the non-Interrail runs were just one-way one-offs while others were part of multi-country Euro-Domino trips (Euro-Domino tickets were single country passes that gave you unlimited rail travel for various numbers of days within a calendar month; the scheme ran from 1990 to 2007 and was in some ways a forerunner of the current Interrail model). Lots of the journeys I discuss were direct A to B journeys on a single train; others involved several changes en route; some took under an hour, some more than two days; and many were on night trains which I've always loved, and I'm very glad to see them currently experiencing quite a renaissance after a relatively long time in the darkness, so to speak – but more of that later too.

One other thing I particularly love about train travel is how it often gives you time and space to think and reflect. So a lot of what follows is also filled with my own musings and thoughts – hence the ramblings in the title. If I'm honest, I think this aspect has been amplified by writing this book in early retirement – leaving work behind, losing both my parents and slowly getting older all seem to have the effect of making you look back on life and what you've done, and where you've been. Maybe less so where you're going... Who was it that said that life can only be understood looking backwards but lived forwards? (Kierkegaard, apparently).

So, if you like a pick-n-mix bag of assorted railway travelogues, peppered with a bit of train history and random personal ramblings, then I hope you'll enjoy reading what follows. There's no plot, no beginning, middle and no end really – so the sections could be read in any order. And although this is definitely a long way from being a 'how-to' rail travel guide (how could anyone ever compete with *The Man in Seat 61*?!), I have included a few thoughts and suggestions that might be useful if you are thinking about travelling abroad by train. Admittedly, some of these are slightly tongue-in-cheek. And even though the sections are all relatively short, non-chronological accounts of different journeys, I hope the sum of all these small parts has added up to something bigger – a personal homage to train travel and the wonderfully scenic and emotional places it can take us to;

a token tribute to all the pleasures, people and stories it connects us with; and a testament to how it can also at times test us and push us to reflect on our lives, ourselves and the world around us.

A

A1 - Amsterdam to Paris – on the Etoile du Nord line

Route: Amsterdam – The Hague – Rotterdam – Roosendaal – Berchem (Antwerp) – Brussels – Mons – St Quentin – Paris

This three-capital journey starting out from Amsterdam is one I've done quite a few times over the years. The first time was on my first ever Interrail trip in 1985. Back then, a night train still left Amsterdam at around 22.00, and ambled along at a snail's pace to give passengers the chance to try and get a bit of sleep before arriving in Paris at what was still a relatively uncivilised hour the next morning. I'd decided to travel overnight to save the expense of accommodation, but after an uncomfortable night shuffling and fidgeting in your seat, you pay the price next day. Suffice it to say it was the last time I ever took the night train on this route. After that I always took one of the daytime services that covered the route in about five hours; today, the high-speed Eurostars do it in just over three.

Thinking back to that first time in 1985, I remember feeling like such an intrepid lone adventurer, taking a night train calling in at three European capitals; a fairly tame undertaking by the standards of many of today's adventurous 'yoof', of course. I also never imagined at the time that I'd end up living and working in Amsterdam just a few years later. That first trip to Amsterdam had made quite an impression on me, I think because in so many ways it was unlike anywhere else I'd ever been. As I walked out of the station (and what a glorious station it is), the sights of the city hit me straight away - the shimmering canals and waterways that permeate the centre, the endless rows of beautiful gabled houses, and of course, the provocatively startling Red Light Area. We're probably far more blasé these days but forty years ago in the pre-internet Mary Whitehouse world, Amsterdam felt like an incredibly edgy, boundary-pushing city. Walking past sex shops, live shows, 'coffee shops' and brothels – and even a Satanic temple at one point – made me feel amazingly adventurous, it didn't matter that I didn't have the nerve to go into any of these places – I was somewhere where it was all happening. And all this seediness offset by beautifully historic surroundings. This couldn't have been further away from the town I grew up in, with its Co-op, betting shop and Berni Inn.

There is of course a far more high-brow cultural side to Amsterdam, with its famous art museums and concert halls, but back then this didn't much appeal (should I be ashamed to say?). I was fascinated by this glimpse into such a different world where anything seemed to go, and by how the slightly twisted glamour and semi-respectable squalor sat comfortably side by side. I tried to capture some of this feeling in a comedy novel I wrote many years later about a disillusioned Black Country teacher who abandons his humdrum life and goes off in search of adventure... and ends up running a sex shop in Amsterdam (*Gerard Philey's Euro-Diary: Quest for a Life* – please forgive the shameless plug).

But back to that night train to Paris: there were lots of fellow Interrailers clearly doing the same as me. Earwigging on their conversations, it was obvious that some Americans a few seats further down had been drawn to Amsterdam's easy access to soft drugs. And by the sound of it, several of them were still enjoying what they'd managed to get hold of ("This is crazy shit, dude, roll me another"). This meant it was a fairly loud carriage, so much so that after a while, a couple of brave Australians made a tentative appeal for some peace and quiet – sadly in vain. By the time the train crossed the border into Belgium, things had calmed down a bit but by then it didn't much matter – it was just impossible to get comfortable and my stiff neck was approaching the terminal phase. When the train finally arrived at the Gare du Nord at ridiculously early o'clock, I'd aged several years and was in no mood to rush round taking in the many splendours Paris had to offer.

But what can you do at that time in a morning? The young me clearly hadn't thought this through very well. After a bit of aimless and grouchy trudging about, I decided to take the metro to Trocadéro for an early view of the Eiffel Tower. By the time I came out of the metro station, I realised sustenance took precedence over sightseeing, so took refuge in the nearest cafe I could find open at that hour. It's hard to say anything about Paris that hasn't already been said but it's very easy to slip into glib generalisation about the city's Bohemian flair – so I might as well jump on the bandwagon. But that said, as I sat in that early morning cafe with a coffee and croissants, watching the unshaved, the lonely and the early risers (I was all three myself), it was nothing short of drama – people's lives quietly playing out at the little wooden tables, dark and tragic, yet impossibly glamorous. Gaulloises and an early brandy; coffee and downward glances; dignified but down and out. Maybe it was nothing of the sort, but *Emily in Paris* this certainly was not; and much as that sophisticated glam-fashion side is part of what the city is about, give me the gritty darkness any day.

This was in fact one of a number of slightly inauspicious arrivals in Paris on the train from Amsterdam. Later on in the 1980s, Margaret and I made the same journey for a short break in the city. We'd heard from someone we knew that there was an accommodation bureau in the Gare du Nord where you could book somewhere to stay on arrival. In the pre-internet age, this seemed like a really useful suggestion. But when we managed to locate said bureau that evening (after an afternoon departure from Amsterdam) we were horrified to see the length of the queue – and even more so to hear (via the message system operating up and down the queue by word of mouth) that everything was fully booked... the bureau was passing on details of vacancies as hotels called to notify them of cancellations. So we waited... and waited... We slowly got closer to the front of the queue, and after several hours (= lifetimes in queuing years) we were offered a room at a reasonable rate in a decent area. Since then, I would never contemplate arriving in a big city without having pre-arranged accommodation, but as so often in life, we end up learning the hard way.

As mentioned, the train service between Amsterdam, Brussels and Paris is now just a three-hour trip on a high-speed Thalys, and even though it took longer in the past, it's always been a well-served route with several direct trains a day, and plenty more if you caught the hourly Amsterdam to Brussels train and changed at Midi/Zuid Station. The most famous of all the Amsterdam-Paris trains has to be the Etoile du Nord (Northern Star). First introduced in 1923, it ran as a fast train between Paris and Brussels only but was extended to Amsterdam from 1927 when it was also upgraded to a luxury service (there are some wonderful posters designed by Cassandre advertising the train from this period). The war led to its suspension for a few years but it was eventually re-launched, and in 1957 it became a first-class only Trans Europe Express (TEE). It was later downgraded as a dual-class international intercity, only to be upgraded yet again in 1987 when it joined the EuroCity category (see J below), which remained the case until it was replaced by the Thalys services that began in 1996. I travelled on it as far as Brussels in the early 90s when it was still the EC Etoile du Nord. SNCF were using 'Inox' carriages for the train at the time – these had previously been used on some TEE routes and the most remarkable thing about them was their startlingly shiny silver livery. Pulling into the station, it made quite an entrance, oozing futuristic style and prestige – outside of sci-fi films, when else have you ever seen a stainless steel train?! But alas, its days are no more; the Eurostar may be fast and fairly stylish itself, but it somehow lacks the class and cachet of the old Etoile du Nord. Deep nostalgic sigh, and many more to follow.

A2 - Amsterdam to Milan – on the Holland Italy Express

Route: Amsterdam – Utrecht – Arnhem – Emmerich – Cologne – Bonn – Mainz – Mannheim – Basle SBB – Lucerne – Gotthard – Chiasso – Como - Milan

The Holland Italy Express was once one of the great express trains connecting northern and southern Europe. Starting life in the 1950s, it ran nightly from Amsterdam to Rome, a journey of around twenty-four hours. After moving eastwards through Holland, it entered Germany near Duisburg before heading down the Rhine into Switzerland at Basle, through the Gotthard Tunnel, and eventually emerging in Italy to continue its southward journey via Milan and Florence. Over the years, the destination was occasionally switched to Ventimiglia on the Italian Riviera (in winter) or the Adriatic resort of Rimini (in summer). At different points en route, through coaches from Hamburg, Dortmund and Frankfurt were added on, making for a very long train by the time it arrived at its destination. By the early 1990s, however, many long-distance international night trains were struggling to compete with cheaper and faster flight options. This train was no exception, and 1991 sadly saw its final year as a cross-continental workhorse. A direct connection between Holland and Italy was briefly re-introduced in 2007 when CityNightLine (CNL – the now disbanded German-owned network of night trains) launched the short-lived Apus service between Amsterdam and Milan.

I'm really glad I managed to travel on the train in the late 1980s. At the time, I was living in Holland, teaching English in a secondary school in Rotterdam (my first 'proper job' since leaving university, and what a baptism of fire that was. I'd need a few more hours in therapy to write any more on that topic so will leave it there). An Irish friend of ours working in Milan had invited us down to stay at half term. Trains then were still very much the most obvious and cheapest travel option, and a direct overnight connection between Amsterdam and Milan made things simple too. So once mid-October arrived, Margaret and I boarded the train and looked forward to a sunny week in milder Italian climes. One of the wonderful things about international trains of this kind was their dazzlingly distinctive appearance as they sidled along the platform – multiple colourful carriages made up of German, Dutch, Swiss and Italian rolling stock. To save on the expense of a sleeping compartment, we'd booked two bunks in a six-berth couchette.

As was/is the custom, couchette compartments doubled up as ordinary seating compartments for the first few hours. When bedtime arrived, the attendant would work their way through the carriage, converting daytime seats into night-time couchette bunks. I've been lucky enough on rare occasions to have a compartment for six all to myself – especially in Eastern Europe in the past, when flashing a few Deutsch Marks could still work wonders. But it was not to be the case this time – the train was jam-packed. I remember looking around the compartment with some relief that none of our co-travellers appeared openly obnoxious – fifteen hours cooped up with strangers can sometimes feel a very long time. Even in the days before pinging mobiles and the like.

One of the things I love about train journeys is that initial frisson of excitement after boarding. Suddenly, there you are – on the way; sitting back, starting to relax, looking out of the window, intrigued and absorbed by the scenery and the lulling rattle of metal on metal (thank you, Kraftwerk; if you know, you know). Just at that point, I remember two Dutch women deciding to shell a seemingly never-ending supply of the smelliest ever boiled eggs (I think it was four in reality – but in a small compartment with the window closed on a chilly October evening.... I'll say no more). To be fair, most people in those days self-catered for the journey. Dining cars weren't always available, and if they were, they were often expensive or over-crowded (or both). If you were lucky, there'd be a mini-bar attendant along at some point with Heinekens and Kit Kats for the price of a modest semi in Surrey.

After a couple of hours, we crossed the German border and arrived at Emmerich. Pre-Schengen, border guards and customs officers still commonly patrolled the trains. I've always found this extremely exciting (maybe I need to get out more). There's something about crossing borders that fills me with wonder – the language often changes, the houses and architecture look slightly different, train staff wear different uniforms, and so on. There's something fascinating and exhilarating about that abruptly tangible shift between two worlds. And on top of that – and this probably comes from watching too many war films as a child – I always relished that slight thrill of danger when the border guards appeared. In my case, I'm glad to say this has been a needless fear, though I've since experienced some rather upsetting scenes for other passengers elsewhere, but more of that later.

The train soon continued its long southward trek through Germany down to the Swiss border, by which time couchettes had all been made up, and our fellow occupants were attempting to sleep... and ignore the lingering aftermath of boiled eggs. I remember my excitement as we pulled into Switzerland – my first time ever – and thinking about the wonderful scenery that would eventually pass by outside. But as this was a night train, sadly none of it would be visible – hey-ho. By the time morning came, we got our first glimpses of a very different looking world – very different from Holland and Germany, that is. Suddenly, golden autumnal sunshine covered the hillsides of the Swiss-Italian border, and before too long, the shores of Lake Como were on us, the nearby Alps bearing gloriously down. I always think it's slightly odd the next morning when you look around the compartment – everyone's bleary-eyed, nobody's at their best, all shuffling past one another clutching wash-bags and toothbrushes. There's something reminiscent of the awkward intimacy of a one-night-stand the morning after (I imagine) – which in a way is exactly what it is, I suppose (without the sex – but who knows?).

Arriving in Milan that morning is something I don't think I'll ever forget. Milan Central is without a doubt my favourite railway station. Ok, it may have been built by Mussolini and his fascists in the 1930s, and it might ooze bombast from every beautiful corner and crevice, but it's amazing, inside and out – grand, over-the-top, imposing; it's not just in your face - it grabs you by the neck and tongues you before you've even been introduced properly. This may not be everyone's reaction of course, but Birmingham New Street it really is not (no disrespect to Birmingham New Street, old version or new). Milan Central is apparently still the biggest railway station in Europe, and looking around it that morning, I had no trouble believing that.

Once outside, Milan itself is perhaps less impressive than its glorious station but that might be being a bit unkind. It's a huge place (Italy's second largest city), and 'the sights' are accordingly spread around the city (the Last Supper fresco, the Sforzesco Castle, La Scala and so on). The cathedral for me has to be its most impressive monument – it rivals the station in scale (it's the third largest religious structure in the world) and campery - like the station, it's just an outrageously over-the-top immensity. The views from the roof were quite amazing, and not just because of what you could see of the city below – as you ambled along the roof, it felt like you were actually walking in the sky among the statues and sculptures that sit atop the spires and pinnacles. This gave the whole experience of being up there a very surreal, ethereal quality that has always stayed with me. On a repeat trip to the city thirty years later, I was hoping to revisit the cathedral roof; the sight of the queue was immediately daunting, however. And when I saw a sign advising of a six hour wait, I instantly abandoned the idea. It strikes me that tourists everywhere these days need immense patience (and pockets), or the good sense to plan and book every trip, visit and experience well in advance. But be that as it may, I'd go back to Milan any day. And it's amazing to think that travelling by rail from London (and Amsterdam) to Milan can now be comfortably done within daylight hours, thanks to high-speed connections via Eurostar and TGV.

A3 - Århus to Copenhagen – on the ferry and Zealand train

Route: Århus – Kalundborg - Holbaek – Roskilde – Copenhagen

Infrastructure improvements over the last few years mean that trains today between Denmark's second and first cities now travel the entire route in just over three hours. Before the Great Belt Fixed Link was completed in 1998 (which enabled a fixed rail and road link between the Danish islands of Funen and Zealand), it was often easier for passengers from central and northern Jutland to catch a ferry from Århus to Kalundborg on Zealand, and take the connecting train from there. Back in 1985, I was spending a few weeks with my then girlfriend who lived in Århus, and this was exactly the route we took when we headed to Copenhagen for a couple of days.

Århus itself is a charming city to wander around – easy-going, pleasant and not too challenging. If it was going on a dating app, that's probably how it would describe itself. Very much a steady Eddy who likes half a pint now and again and a walk in the park of a Sunday. I don't mean to demean it in any way at all (or middle-aged chaps like me whose ideal weekend I've just described) but it's not exactly Paris, Istanbul or Copenhagen for that matter, and nor does it need to be. Anyway, I liked it very much, and the nearby open air museum village (Den Gamle By – the first of its kind in the world) is an absolute gem of a visit.

But back to 1985 – we caught the bus down to the Århus ferry terminal and were soon on the boat for the morning crossing to Zealand, which took around three hours. On a sunny August day, this was a wonderful way to spend the morning, relaxing in deck chairs set out on deck (I suppose that's how they got their name but this was the first time I'd ever seen them in their natural setting). And as the ferry was part of Denmark's integrated transport system, the cost of the crossing was included in my Interrail ticket, which I thought was brilliant. The waters were calm, the sun was shining, the beers were flowing, and I was en route to Copenhagen – what was there not to like? The relaxation was especially welcome as we'd spent the preceding couple of days at the Skanderborg Music Festival just outside Århus – the Danish equivalent of Glastonbury. To be honest, music festivals have never been my sort of thing. Much as I love music, I can do without the mud, the queuing for the toilets, the bad nights trying to sleep in a tent, and everything else that goes with it. Getting repeatedly wedged under pogoing Scando armpits doing their thing to Status Quo (the headline act) I definitely did not need.

Eventually, we docked in the port of Kalundborg at the western end of the Danish island of Zealand, and boarded the train for Copenhagen (situated at the eastern end) – a journey of just under two hours. I popped on Malene's walkman and remember listening to the song Nattog (night train) by the Danish band Marquis de Sade – an incredibly mellow electro 80s song that beautifully evokes a sense of the hypnotic tranquillity of train travel (well worth YouTubing). In fact I think I nodded off for a while, and came back round to gently rolling meadows and fields which set the scene for the rest of the journey. The train stopped briefly in Roskilde, which I was told holds yet another famous open air music festival (I didn't say anything), and soon after we pulled into Copenhagen Central Station.

I haven't been back to the city since those few days in 1985 but my memories of it are still vivid. It reminded me of Amsterdam in terms of the overall vibe – laid back, historic and certainly impressive. The word people bandy about today is 'hygge', the Danish concept of cosy conviviality, and I'd definitely go along with that description. We did all the usual tourist stuff – the Tivoli Gardens, the Amalienborg Palace, the Little Mermaid, took in the city views from the top of the 17th Century Round Tower, and so on. It's startling to think that it's almost forty years ago, but that's one of the strange things about getting older, if you're lucky enough to be able to –

the weirdly contradictory sense of distance/proximity between your past and present. But enough maudlin reflection... I'd absolutely love to go back to Copenhagen, and had better not leave it another forty years.

Train travel thoughts A

Avoid passengers with boiled eggs, if you can.

Make sure you've got enough food and drink on night trains, as you can't always guarantee they'll be available for purchase.

If you really want to see the Swiss Alps, don't travel through them overnight.

Consider pre-booking any must-see visits on your list to avoid disappointment/queuing/back ache.

It's rarely a good idea waiting till you get there to book accommodation.

Don't put off till next year (or forty years) journeys that you could do this year.

B

B1 - Budapest to Bucharest – on the Orient Express

Route: Budapest Keleti – Szolnok - Bekescaba – Lököshaza – Curtici – Arad – Sibiu – Brasov – Sinaia – Ploesti Vest - Bucharest

The first thing I should say is – no, not *that* Orient Express. For most people, the mention of these two words immediately brings to mind thoughts of luxury travel, glamour, Agatha Christie, murder – you get the idea. The aforementioned author is of course largely responsible for this, but technically, that train was the 'Simplon Orient Express', a long-defunct service from Calais and Paris via Yugoslavia to Istanbul. The history of both trains is long and complex; indeed, lots of books have been written about the various versions of the Orient Express, and I don't intend to revisit them here. Suffice it to say that for many years (for well over a hundred years from the 1880s, in fact), a very unglamorous workaday service called the Orient Express sat quietly in the European timetables, covering the 2600 km two-night journey from Paris to Bucharest and back several times a week (eventually shortened to Budapest, then further truncated to Vienna; and for the last few years of its life, it only ran between Strasbourg and Vienna). In its final years on the full Paris to Bucharest stretch, it was far from a luxury train – just an ordinary service transporting ordinary folk. In fact, calling it ordinary would often be something of a compliment, as the two-night trip was in most people's experience a bit of a trial – dining cars often absent or available only for short stretches, basic sleeping accommodation, filthy toilets, limited running water, long delays en route and at borders... need I go on?

Despite this reputation, I still thought it was worth travelling on to get to the Romanian capital after a few days' stay in Hungary. After all, it was a direct overnight connection, how bad could it really be? Maybe it was just a bit of a bad boy who'd been the victim of negative labelling? Time would tell; and indeed it did. But more of that in a moment. As it wasn't due to arrive in Budapest till after eight in the evening, it meant we had another full day to enjoy in the capital. Knowing that we needed to keep going till then, we decided to take it easy, so made our way up to Buda Castle. We'd spent a couple of days previously exhausting ourselves taking in the main sights on foot (the parliament, the wonderful Chain Bridge, and so on), so a gentle wander in and around the sprawling castle grounds in lovely weather was a relaxing way to while away the hours. The views looking down over the Danube are stunning, and there are plenty of places to sit quietly with a drink and a book. I must admit that from up close, the castle was looking a bit tired and the worse for wear (it may have had a facelift since). Having seen it previously from some distance down in the city, especially when lit up at night, it looked amazing.

But then I suppose many of us, myself included, look a bit better from a distance, and I shouldn't really be judging – how good would I look up close at 300 years old? Anyway, the hours effortlessly slipped by, and by the time we'd had our evening meal, it was time to head back to the wonderfully impressive Keleti station and find out how bad (or good) the Orient Express really was.

Actually, it wasn't too bad – if you expect the worst, things rarely end up bad as you'd think (the pessimist's creed, and one that seems to come naturally to me). We had a compartment for the two of us in the Romanian Railways sleeping car – so at least we had the luxury of privacy on what turned out to be a sixteen-hour journey (just a slight three hour delay but who's rushing?). The toilets did live up to their reputation but they could have been a lot worse, especially considering the train had already been en route for a day by the time it reached Budapest, having travelled via Strasbourg, Stuttgart, Munich, Salzburg and Vienna. In fact, on the return leg of this journey, they were far worse, and I have to own up to it partly being my fault – as a result of a nasty dose of food poisoning that made its presence felt rather dramatically a few hours after boarding, I found myself spending several hours of the return trip on the loo, in what was actually one of my worst ever train experiences – sitting on a filthy toilet in the middle of a hot night, the world falling out of my bottom (apologies to the faint of heart), feeling like death (not even death warmed up), flies buzzing relentlessly round my head (why do they do this?), and Hungarian/Romanian border guards angrily banging on the toilet door demanding to see my passport – not my finest or most dignified hour, and I won't describe the looks of horror and disdain on the guards' faces when I finally gave in and opened the door. When I've had rough times since then, this experience has become a personal benchmark of badness – I can usually say, 'Well, at least it's not as bad as that night on the Orient Express'.

Returning to the Budapest-Bucharest trip, however, it was otherwise a pretty decent journey, delays apart. Relatively quiet and little disturbed after leaving Hungary, the train rattled along nicely. By morning, Transylvania was approaching. Like many people of my age in the UK, Hammer films were a staple part of my childhood; Dracula and vampires had become etched into my DNA as a kid because of my TV diet-cum-fascination, so the prospect of travelling through the whole of Transylvania was an exciting one. The Carpathians did not disappoint – rugged hills and mountains loomed down on us, and at one point, a distant hilltop cross inevitably brought to mind images of local peasants doing their best to keep the evil Count and his cronies at bay. I was desperately hoping to catch a glimpse of a castle, but Castle Bran (the one most associated – rightly or wrongly - with Vlad the Impaler) could sadly not be spotted from the train, though we did stop briefly in nearby Brasov (a wonderful medieval town I visited some years later).

Arriving for the first time in Bucharest was another unforgettable experience. It goes without saying that Romania had suffered terribly under Ceausescu – poverty was everywhere, and the desperation that goes with it was more than evident at the central station, the Gara de Nord. As we stepped off the train, it initially seemed fairly quiet, if not a little disconcerting to see armed guards patrolling the platform. But as soon as we walked out of the station, we realised why they were there. Coming out through the main exit was like jumping into an unwashed and uncontrolled mass of beggars, pickpockets, traders and ragamuffins – an unsettling chaos that somehow evoked both revulsion and sympathy. With our wits fully charged and our heads down, we managed to get through this manic melee and into a taxi. On a repeat visit some years later, by which point the country had been an EU member for some time, it was heartening to see how much better things appeared to be for ordinary Romanians, and how much Bucharest had improved, even if some of its charms were still a little rough round the edges - and actually all the more charming for it. It was much easier to see why it had once been called the Paris of the East, the elegance of its architecture once more shining through the tarnish of yesteryear.

Rail connections between Budapest and Bucharest have also improved a lot in recent years. Starting in Vienna, the

Dacia Express leaves Budapest late evening, arriving in the Romanian capital the next afternoon. An earlier and generally more comfortable Ister service leaves early evening, arriving late morning the next day (when on time). There's also an afternoon departure on the Muntenia reaching Bucharest the next morning. The Traianus, named after the Roman Emperor Trajan, just about manages to connect both capitals within the same day, leaving at around 7.00 and arriving not far off midnight (delays permitting again). But sadly, the Orient Express has long since been consigned to history....

B2 – (Newcastle -) Bergen to Voss on a Norwegian intercity

Route: Bergen – Arna – Vaksdal – Stanghelle – Bolstadøyri – Evanger – Seimsgrend – Voss

Margaret and I had arrived in Bergen on the overnight ferry from Newcastle. I say overnight but it had taken the best part of twenty-four hours, so there was plenty of daytime taken up too. This was in 1998 when the ferry still ran. Sadly, after 140 years, it ceased operation in 2008, though I've read there are plans to reopen the route in a couple of years. Even though we crossed the North Sea in summer, it was still pretty rough and we spent quite a bit of time lying down in our cabin trying to pretend we were perfectly ok and that the awful head-spinning and stomach gyrations would soon disappear. Fortunately there were hours of relative calm in between these bouts, which meant we were able to enjoy some of the onboard entertainment in the bar. This included bilingual bingo which caused mass hilarity at times, particularly when the numbers announced in Norwegian sounded almost exactly like the English versions with a slightly comedic accent (e.g forty-two = førtito); there was something about the mass British sniggering that evolved into widespread guffawing that got everyone going, but I suspect you maybe had to be there.

This continued when some of the crew did a session on the various wares available for purchase: "Weh hav somm exquissite ornaments availøble, beautifully fashøned from the bessst quality pewter, a mosst refined and sophisticated material which we Norwegians call 'tinn.'" Again, I think it was the sound of Brits snorting into their pints which prompted infectious belly laughs. Talking of pints, there was widespread disgruntlement (again, among the Brits) about the cost of drinks from the bar. A chap from Halifax sitting nearby was charged close to £10 for a pint of lager - "I couldn't believe it!" he said – "I let out the Yorkshire war cry – 'ow much?!!? No wonder the Vikings crossed the North Sea!"

Despite everything, we managed to get a reasonable night's sleep and the next morning the ferry called first at Stavanger before continuing north towards Bergen, following the coast quite closely, which meant stunning views for several hours. We arrived in Bergen mid-afternoon, and what a lovely city it is. Surrounded by mountains wherever you look (apart from out to sea), the views are magnificent. The old harbour area at Bryggen is a colourful collection of wooden Hanseatic buildings, and a charming place to wander round or sit with a beer (once you've got the second mortgage sorted). We were travelling on to a town called Voss further inland, so made our way to the railway station. From the outside, it looked a little austere and uninviting with its dark chunky brickwork, but once inside, its glass ceiling completely cancelled out this impression. It would only be a ninety minute journey of around 85 km, but it was along one of the oldest railway lines in Norway, the Bergen/Voss line, which continues on to Oslo. Many people describe this as one of the greatest rail journeys on the planet, and it's not difficult to see why.

We soon found a couple of seats and were immediately impressed by the spacious interior design, the standard of cleanliness and the degree of comfort. Waiting for the train to depart felt like the same anticipation I experience at the start of a film in the cinema. Moments later, the train pulled out and began its gradual ascent out through the suburbs and into the rugged, mountainous landscape, hugging at times the deep fjords that pierce and penetrate the Norwegian coastline. For such a gentle and peace-loving nation, it's ironic that much of the landscape they live in is so dauntingly wild and beautifully forbidding. At certain points, the views were genuinely breathtaking, and I now regret that we didn't take advantage of being near the Flåm-Myrdal heritage railway to see the even more spectacular sights which that line offers – another time. Given the mountainous terrain we were travelling through, this inevitably meant that at times the only views available were of the walls of some very lengthy tunnels hewn out of Precambrian granite - less picturesque but undeniably impressive. Some of them were very long indeed – in fact, the Trollkona Tunnel, at close to 9 km, is the longest tunnel on the entire stretch between Bergen and Oslo. This was quite a trip but, looking round at our fellow passengers, I was surprised that most of the locals barely glanced out of the window – they munched on sandwiches, chatted softly or sat quietly with a magazine. I found it hard to believe that travelling through such amazing scenery could ever become so mundane that it would play second fiddle to a cheese and ham bap.

And so it continued for the rest of the journey - tunnel, jaw-dropping scenery, tunnel, staggering views, tunnel, gasps of delight, tunnel.... you get the idea. It wasn't long before we arrived in Voss' unassuming little station. Beautifully situated between the Sogne and Hardanger fjords, the town is apparently known globally as the 'extreme sports village' but it was more the 'admiring the scenery while mooching about' that we were there for, and very nice it was too. I've never understood why people want to hurtle down mountains risking life and limb, but each to their own of course. I was quite happy taking my time viewing some of the area's immense waterfalls, its wild, fast-flowing rivers, and experiencing the heart-racing challenge of spending £12 on a glass of wine while smiling gratefully.

Train travel thoughts B

Make sure you always have a supply of imodium or similar on long journeys.

Money belts are always a good idea for your cash and documents.

Don't try to cram absolutely everything into your tour; it's good to leave something for another visit.

C

C1 - Cologne to Geneva on the Switzerland Express (Schweiz Express)

Route: Cologne – Bonn – Mainz – Mannheim – Heidelberg – Basle SBB – Biel/Bienne – Lausanne - Geneva

On this particular trip, I'd travelled down from northern Germany during the day and had a good few hours to re-acquaint myself with Cologne. Cologne has always felt a bit special to me. Having done German at school, I remember learning about how badly it had been bombed during the Second World War, and can still vividly recall textbook pictures of its wonderful cathedral standing proud among the city rubble. It's strange how particular images can stay with you, and the impression they make when you actually see them for the first time in real life. This can sometimes be sadly underwhelming in reality, but occasionally quite the opposite. And that was absolutely the case for me when first en route from Ostend to southern Germany as a teenager. I changed at Cologne and had some time before my connection. As I walked out of the station, I was immediately confronted by the cathedral's towering presence. I think part of its power has something to do with its potency as a symbol of resilience. As I arrived there for the first time, full of teenage angst and turmoil, and saw this mighty edifice that had been through so much still standing there, its message was clear to me – don't worry, this too will pass. Needless to say, I've ended up with quite a soft spot for Cologne and its cathedral, and I'm sure many of us end up attaching our affections to particular places and buildings that we come across at certain points in our lives. So, spending a few hours wandering around the cathedral and walking along the banks of the Rhine was a welcome repeat pleasure. After something to eat, it was soon time to head back into the bustling station to board the Schweiz Express.

For many years, the Switzerland Express was an important nightly connection between northern and central Europe. The main route ran from Holland, down the Rhine and into Switzerland at Basle. At different times of the year, there were direct through coaches travelling to other Swiss destinations such as Bern, Brig, Interlaken, Zurich, Chur and Chiasso. Through coaches also ran from Dortmund to pick up passengers from the major urban centres in the Rhine-Ruhr conurbation. In some ways, this service fared better than many other international night trains. It survived the European night train cull of the early 1990s, running as the Schweiz Express until the 2000s. When CNL took charge of night operations, an Amsterdam – Zurich/Brig 'Pegasus' service was resumed between 2007 and 2016. At the time of writing, it's good to see that Nightjet have again reinstated the service, running nightly from Amsterdam to Basle and Zurich (see V1 Vienna to Gdansk for more on Nightjet).

Like a good many international trains of old, the Dutch departure point for the Schweiz Express was Amsterdam, which it had left at around 20.00 that evening. By the time it pulled into Cologne after 23.00, it was already fairly full, and I was very aware of disturbing the other passengers when I tried my best not to make any noise as I got into my couchette berth with the lights off. However hard you try of course, you always manage to knock something off a bunk when mauling with your case or rucksack. I've realised this is one of those things that nobody wins at, and despite your best efforts, you end up annoying someone and incurring general grumbling. Sorry.

This particular night journey always sticks in my mind as being one of the most uncomfortable couchette journeys I've experienced (and there's quite a list). The compartment was hot and full. There was a snoring competition going on. It seemed like there'd been a pre-arranged rota for the other occupants to take turns in exiting and returning to the compartment. Absolutely fair enough of course, but the noise of the compartment door opening has always pushed me to a compulsive check-and-clutch routine – passport, tickets, wallet. Over the years, I've heard lots of stories about thieves on night trains, and these tales have always stayed with me. I once had a fairly close shave myself – but more on that later. Putting all this together, a peaceful night's sleep was not on the agenda (something to think about for anyone mulling over the choice between couchette and sleeping compartment). So by the time the train pulled into Switzerland at its final destination, Basle SBB, at 6.00 in the morning, I was far from at my best, but hey, I was in Switzerland! How many mornings could I say that? Shambling off with the rest of the night train zombies, it was an easy change for the early morning connection to Geneva – a journey of around three hours via Lausanne.

As mentioned above, one of the things I've learned since is that if you can, it's worth shelling out that bit more for a sleeping compartment to get a proper overnight rest. Unless you're a very easy devil-may-care sleeper, the only advantage of a couchette berth is being able to lie flat rather than sitting up all night. And that's about it. As it was, I arrived in Geneva thinking I never wanted to go anywhere ever again, feeling like I'd been up for three weeks. I trudged to the B & B I'd booked and was pleased they were happy to let me check in ahead of the official time – always a relief. After a few hours' sleep, all was well again, and I was off to do a bit of sightseeing, humming the theme tune to the 60s/70s TV series, *The Champions* - a programme that made quite an impression on me and lots of others who grew up in the 70s. The opening shot featured a stunning view of the city's famous jet fountain (The Champions' HQ being in Geneva), and clapping eyes on it for the first time was thrilling, particularly against a warm blue sky. So thrilling, in fact, that I momentarily forgot feeling like a discarded scarecrow among the Euro-city slickers, as I was transported back to that enthralled childhood wonder, seeing my three favourite super-agents standing there all exotic, gorgeous and adventurous. Geneva has plenty to offer the more culturally demanding tourist too of course, but I was happy just indulging these childhood memories. I realise yet again how some of my happiest travel memories have involved a happy sense of linking back to some childhood association; maybe experiencing these connections in some small way validates us, confirming our past and present. I'm not sure I entirely understand it but I've experienced it several times, and it's always wonderful.

C2 - Cambridge to Amsterdam – on The European et al.

Route: Cambridge – Ely – Bury St. Edmunds – Ipswich – Harwich Parkeston Quay – Hook of Holland - The Hague - Leiden - Amsterdam

Ordinarily, this would be a fairly unremarkable trip but surprisingly, it ended up being one of the weirdest ever rail journeys of my life. It was meant to be a straightforward weekend break to Amsterdam. I'd done the trip from Cambridge several times before and it had always been uneventful. But then there's always that one time – this time in 1987. I got on an early evening train at Cambridge station for what was normally a steady run across East Anglia to the coast to pick up the night boat to the Hook at Harwich. The first sign of trouble was the scheduled departure time coming and going.... after about twenty minutes, a guard came through the carriage and announced the delay was down to waiting for five passengers who'd mistakenly boarded the wrong train to come back to Cambridge and get on this one. I know I might have seen it differently if I'd been one of the five (whoever they were) but curmudgeon that I am, it just seemed a bit ridiculous to delay an entire train for the sake of a few people who'd made a mistake. Then I did something apparently outrageous – I tutted audibly. At this, the guard made a beeline for me and let forth an extensive torrent of abuse that seemed completely out of a proportion to a solitary tut. When I realised it wasn't a wind-up, I made the mistake of responding – politely but firmly, I should add. Somehow, it ended up degenerating into a full-blown (verbal) confrontation, during which every other passenger firmly fixed their gaze on the floor or their book. Eventually, the guard walked away when the five missing passengers arrived, and off we went at last.

It was then just a short run to Ely where I had to change to pick up 'The European' boat train (see U - Utrecht to the Hook of Holland for more on named British boat trains of the past) on its way down from Edinburgh to Harwich. I was worried I might have missed the connection given the previous delay, but as luck would have it, it was also delayed. And delayed... Then, after an hour, it arrived – trouble with the brakes, apparently. Once we got to Bury St. Edmunds, the engine failed. A new engine would be driven over from Cambridge, we were told, and we weren't to worry about missing the ferry as officials in Harwich had been informed. Praise be, I thought. Shortly after this, another announcement: passengers for the ferry were to alight and make their way to the taxi rank where we'd be taken to a hotel in Ipswich for the night at British Rail's expense – the ferry had decided it couldn't wait after all. Mass grumbling and despondency ensued. I'd wanted to tut very loudly but didn't dare.

It didn't get any better when I realised solo travellers would be room sharing – and fortune smiled on me yet again, putting me with a flatulent chain-smoking businessman from Buxton. He swapped the smoking for snoring when we went to bed (two singles, at least), but the flatulence sadly continued. The next morning at breakfast, we were rounded up by an overbearing elderly woman called May, travelling with her mild-mannered middle-aged son and daughter. She remembered us from the train and screechingly corralled us all to sit together at the same long table – 'Buxton' and me, a Dutch woman with her young son, two gay blokes from Blackpool, and a 'Keith and Candice-Marie' couple – it was gradually turning into a Mike Leigh play. The corralling continued when we were taxied on to Harwich for the day crossing

– and where we were dismayed to learn that the night boat had in fact waited the previous evening – clearly, wires had got crossed and gormlessness prevailed yet again. The unnecessary expense of taxis and hotel accommodation for possibly a hundred passengers doesn't bear thinking about (silent and private tut).

May's corralling carried on once we boarded the ferry and were rounded up to sit with her and 'the kids' in the bar. Everyone's discomfort was palpable but I don't think anyone, myself included, quite knew how to break away in the face of such eccentric but well-intentioned persistence – it was just easier to obey orders and make the best of the social awkwardness. I did try at one point using a visit to duty-free as an excuse...but when I ventured back into a different corner of the bar an hour or so later, May hauled me straight back into the fold with a raucous "Cooey! Cooey! We're still over here!" And on it went, all the way to the Hook. To be fair, they were a nice bunch of people, it just felt really odd that we were being treated like a school party on the move. Ridiculously, there was no change by the time we reached Holland – we were all heading for Amsterdam, and so ended up sitting together, either side of the aisle on the old yellow 'hondekop' (dog head) boat train to the Central Station, where we finally went our separate ways after a lengthy round of awkward good-byes. All in all, it had been a very strange but memorable twenty-four hours. I've been very careful to refrain from tutting in public ever since – you never know what dark and weird forces it might unleash.

Train travel thoughts C

Do your best to get into a couchette compartment quietly, but you can only do your best.

Think carefully about the choice between couchette and sleeper, especially if you definitely need a good night's sleep.

If you live in East Anglia and are thinking of travelling to Holland, have a look at the Dutch Flyer – you can travel from anywhere within the Greater Anglia service area to the Hook of Holland for a one-ticket price.

Never tut in front of train personnel.

D

D1 - Duisburg to Innsbruck – on the Luna night train

Route: Duisburg – Dusseldorf – Cologne – Bonn – Wurzburg – Ingolstadt – Munich - Innsbruck

After a few days visiting friends who lived near Duisburg, my plan was to head south to Austria to continue my Interrail trip, so I booked a couchette berth on the Luna night train leaving at 22.45. When I got on board I was pleased to see there was only one other person in the six-berth compartment, even though this was July. Sometimes you could be really lucky – back then at least. These days, trains seem full to capacity regardless of day, time of year or where you're going. Have rail companies just got better at (or more ruthless about) efficiently matching demand to capacity? Or is it overtourism? I honestly don't know but my hunch is it's a bit of both – more folks on the move combined with a 'cram-'em-in' business model. Whatever the case, it felt like luxury having a bit of space and privacy, and the relative peace and quiet, combined with minimal interruptions and the absence of border controls meant a fairly decent night was on the cards for once.

In my experience, on the rare occasions I've found myself sharing a couchette compartment with just one or two other people, it can go one of two ways – the other person is either the type who has won awards in successive years for contributions to endless and mindless chat, or they're a total sociopath, hell bent on avoiding conversation and eye contact at all costs. Ok, there might be the odd person in between who strikes a happy medium, but by and large, it's type 1 or 2. I should say that I tend to fit into the second category, especially if it's late and getting some decent kip is a priority (when isn't it?). It's a strange thing really, as train conversations with strangers can often be a lot of fun, and part of me thinks we should always seek them out when travelling, in order to enrich the experience. On the other hand, my inner curmudgeon is more than happy to withdraw into myself and drop the shutters. There's an unattributed quote I've seen a number of times on social media:

> The hypocrisy of being human; the constant tug between solitude and company, the desire to love so desperately and simultaneously be detached from it all, of wanting everything and wanting nothing.

It possibly overstates things a little but these sentiments certainly resonate with me, especially in couchette compartments late at night. On this particular journey, my fellow traveller was also of the second type, so peace and quiet was definitely the order of the day/night. Thinking back, the only thing I remember about my co-traveller was that she was a woman. At the time, I thought nothing at all of this – after all, people very rarely undress in a couchette compartment (in my experience, at least). But it strikes me that we live more and more in a climate of tension, with an acute awareness of vulnerability and safety concerns at every turn. As things stand at the moment, mixed couchettes are still the norm, but I wonder for how much longer. Women-only couchettes are in fact widely available these days. I can understand why some would opt for that, but in a way, it seems a slightly sad reflection on how things have developed in society, and at some level a recognition of our increasing mistrust and suspicion of one another.

But back to the train - the Luna night service ran from the top to bottom of Germany for many years. Off and on over the years, its starting point was Norddeich Mole on the German North Sea coast of East Frisia. There were ferries from the port to and from the East Frisian Islands, and the train would take passengers down the length of West Germany to the Bavarian capital, Munich. In 1995, I remember that the train started in Duisburg (in other periods it ran from Münster, slightly further to the north), though the full-length service resumed for a time in subsequent years. At the time of writing, travellers would now have to get to Cologne to pick up the connecting Nightjet service from Brussels to Munich and Innsbruck. Until fairly recently, a private German rail company ran night trains between northern and southern Germany on the Alpen Sylt Night Express. Various services ran from Sylt in northern Germany via Hamburg and Cologne to such destinations as Munich and Salzburg. Current financial constraints have sadly ended up making these trains unviable for the time being.

In the past, travellers from the Rhine-Ruhr region had lots of options for travelling direct to Munich and beyond overnight. Until the late 1980s, the Austria Express collected passengers from the Hook of Holland and later Amsterdam via Dusseldorf and Cologne to Munich and on to Salzburg and Villach/Klagenfurt in Austria, while the Allgäu Express started in Dortmund and headed via Cologne to Munich and Innsbruck. The Austria Express was redubbed the Bavaria Night Express in the 1990s, with direct carriages from both Ostend and Amsterdam but still following the same route down via Cologne to Munich. Daytime services have always been plentiful on this particular route, with many inter-city and ICE trains offering speedy and regular connections.

Following some decent sleep, I was roused by a knock on the compartment door – the train would soon be pulling into Munich. Sometimes there's nothing better than a solid kip and a totally unremarkable journey where everything goes according to plan, and this was exactly one of those times. The train was on time, it was a sunny morning, I felt reasonably refreshed – what more can you ask for? Soon enough, I was stepping off the train at 7.15, looking to see what platform my connecting train to Innsbruck left from. By 7.30, I was on board, comfortably seated and admiring the last bit of beautiful

Bavarian scenery rolling by outside. Again, one of the great things about travelling overnight is that feeling the next morning that you really are somewhere else. I know that sounds totally obvious, and it may not always be the case, but I find that contrast wonderful. The previous evening had seen views of Germany's northern industrial sprawl around Duisburg; admittedly, a modern and spruced up version of what was quite a depressing industrial landscape at one point in history, but an urban scenario all the same. But now it was green rolling hills, forests, Alps soaring in the distance and fast flowing rivers, all saying, "You are no longer where you were".

There are two train routes from Munich to Innsbruck — the first one is the faster EuroCity route that comes with a supplement because of the speed and greater on-board comfort. It is certainly not an ugly route but is definitely less picturesque than the slower journey via Garmisch-Partenkirchen and Mittenwald that I'd definitely recommend, and that's the route I travelled that morning. This was my first ever visit to Austria and it brought to mind all the scenic stereotypes you'd hope for. As the train uneventfully crossed into the Austrian Tyrol, breathtaking views abounded from every angle, and after a gentle couple of hours, it was time to head off and explore the wonderful and historic city of Innsbruck.

I think it'd be very hard not to fall in love with Innsbruck. From wherever you are in the city, the views all around are spectacular, the mountains bearing down from every angle and providing a stunning backdrop to the city's various monuments and buildings. The old town is impressively quaint, and a marvellous place to mooch around. The river Inn runs right through the city centre, and staring down at it from a bridge, I was completely transfixed. This might sound a bit pathetic but I'd never seen water that colour before – an Alpine greenish blue. And the terrific speed it was moving at was genuinely hypnotic. Maybe I'm easily entertained, I don't know, but compared to the steady sluggish brown flow (sadly browner than ever these days, but I won't get into that business, so to speak) that you see in the majority of English towns, this was truly mesmerising. I was a bit taken aback at one point when an elderly woman stopped to ask me if I was ok. I think she thought I was contemplating throwing myself in. I explained I was just enjoying watching the water, at which point she semi-scowled and made a quick get-away, no doubt thinking I wasn't quite right; which is possibly true. I carried on staring at the Inn for a few minutes, contemplating her contradictory reaction – supportive of someone who might be suicidal but dismissive of potentially borderline eccentricity. I may of course be totally over-thinking this. But whatever the case – Innsbruck is an absolute gem of a city, and I think I'm overdue a return.

D2 – Dortmund to Liège – on EC Molière

Route: Dortmund – Bochum – Essen – Dusseldorf – Cologne – Aachen – Verviers – Liège

This was a trip I did in the late 1980s. I'd gone to Dortmund to visit the huge German Rail depot at nearby Witten. At the time, all unused destination signs from the whole of Germany were sent back there for reworking or recycling (even in those days), and for a fee you could arrange a visit to relieve them of redundant stock. Again, I appreciate this is a niche source of thrills but it was railwayana heaven for me. After a successful visit, I'd decided to stay a night and explore Dortmund, a place I'd never previously been to. Without demeaning it, I think it's fair to say Germany has more attractive cities but that doesn't mean it has little to offer. It's a huge city, the biggest in Westphalia, with a hugely significant industrial heritage. Since the demise of much of its heavy industry, it's successfully reinvented itself as a vibrant centre of commerce. It's a big name in the world of football too, of course, and that's no doubt why the National German football museum is based there (not a thing on my list, but each to their own, and I'm the last person to be impugning other people's interests). I enjoyed strolling round the old market square, and like lots of big German cities, it's never dull, even though it might not be the most handsome boy (or girl/non-binary) in town. There was plenty of life, a buzzing atmosphere, and lively pubs and restaurants, so I was more than happy to stay for a night.

From a railway point-of-view, it's always been an extremely important transport hub. And its position at the eastern end of the Rhine-Ruhr region means it's the perfect departure/destination point for national and international services – moving south-west out of Dortmund means picking up nearly all the major North Rhine Westphalian cities (Bochum, Essen, Dusseldorf, Cologne, and so on) before heading down to Bonn, Frankfurt, Stuttgart and Munich, etc. Back in the late 80s, it was probably the country's premier departure point, with a huge number of international and national services starting out from there, and of course many more stopping off en route. The following table shows a small snapshot of services with Dortmund as departure point in the late 80s/early 90s:

Services from Dortmund to:	Train name
Oberstdorf	Allgäu
Munich	Bacchus, Friedrich Schiller, Gutenberg, etc
Koblenz	Beethoven
Salzburg, Klagenfurt/Graz/Ljubljana	Blauer Enzian
Milan, Genoa, Sestri Levante	Carlo Magno
Vienna, Budapest	Franz Liszt

Athens, Sofia, Istanbul	Hellas Istanbul Express
Port Bou (Spanish border)	Hispania
Innsbruck, Verona, Milan	Leonardo da Vinci
Liège, Paris	Molière
Innsbruck	Vorarlberg Express
Nuremberg	Westfalen
Zagreb, Belgrade	Yugoslavia Express

I travelled on one of these on my way to Belgium the next day – the EC Molière train, which was one of the busy early morning departures before 7.00. The Molière itself has quite an interesting history. It used to be a TEE service called *Paris-Ruhr* – a bit unimaginative as names go; but when it was downgraded from TEE to 'D train' (i.e. ordinary express) in 1973, its name was arguably upgraded to that of the 17th Century French dramatist. From 1983 - 86, the service was extended beyond Dortmund to Hamburg and Copenhagen, creating an additional Paris to Copenhagen through service, complete with couchettes and sleepers. In 1986, it even conveyed a Russian sleeping car from Moscow for the final stretch of its journey from Dortmund to Paris. Then in 1987, it was further upgraded as a EuroCity service. Alongside the EC Gustave Eiffel and Parsifal, it thus became one of three daily EC services between Paris and the Rhine Ruhr region. In 1993, there was another name change, this time to that of the influential Belgian chansonnier, Jacques Brel, a name which it kept until 1997 when it was finally replaced by the unnamed high-speed Thalys service.

The early departure was principally aimed at attracting business people from the region's cities, enabling them to reach Paris by early afternoon. It certainly seemed like a sensible idea, as the train was far from empty even at that time of day. Glancing round, I marvelled at my fellow travellers – smart, kempt and fresh, reading the financial dailies in French and German, daintily breakfasting on wholesome fare; I sat there, barely awake/alive, sporting my dragged-through-a-hedge-backwards look with a can of Coke and a Mars Bar. Though there were some hushed conversations, it was also remarkably quiet – something that we very rarely ever get these days on a train at any time of day, with mobile phones ringing constantly, and most folk happy to share their one-sided conversations or music with all present.

The train moved quietly and efficiently through the Ruhr, and after an hour or so we stopped in Dusseldorf's immense main station. I always have to think of the Kraftwerk song *Trans Europe Express* when passing through the station there because of the line (one of the few in the song):

> From station to station, back to Dusseldorf City, meet Iggy Pop and David Bowie.

Bowie was apparently a huge fan of the band and had worked with them in the city in the 1970s. As with lots of things Bowie-related, it added a sense of glamour and mystique to arriving at the station, though I'm not sure to what extent that was shared by the ordinary Germans just going about their day-to-day business that morning. It's a quirky coincidence that the train's later name change should echo another of Bowie's big influences – Jacques Brel. Once out of Dusseldorf, Cologne and Aachen soon followed, and in what seemed like no time at all we were heading for the Belgian border and stopping in Welkenraedt.

Around three hours and several semi-snoozes after leaving Dortmund, the train arrived in Liège's main station, Guillemins. Since 2009, it's been housed in an impressively futuristic building like something out of a sci-fi film but back in the 80s, it was still a pretty uninspiring concrete job. I wanted to see if they had any old signs going spare as it's long been an important rail hub; over the years, there have been direct connections from Liège to places as far afield as Stockholm, Warsaw, Moscow and Genoa. But that particular morning, my enquiries were received with about as much enthusiasm as an unexplained air bubble in a public swimming pool.

The station is also quite a distance from the city centre, so I used a locker for my case and decided to stretch my legs.

I'd been through the city lots of times on trains to Germany from Ostend but had never got off and looked round, so it was nice having the opportunity to explore a bit more. It might not have the immediate wow-factor of Bruges or Ghent but it is a really lovely city – and the capital of Belgium's Wallonia region. Situated on the River Meuse, it was a much bigger city than I'd expected it to be. Once I got to Place St. Lambert, the elegant square in the city centre, I stopped for a coffee and admired the views all around across to the cathedral and town hall.

After a steady saunter around, I decided to brave what for me is the city's most impressive 'sight,' the Montagne de Bueren – a nearly 400-step stairway, flanked by little houses and buildings all the way up – quite a sight to behold from the bottom. I took my time climbing up, disparaging the health fanatics under my breath (the little I had) as they ran up and down, flaunting their fitness and showing off in their lycra. Once I reached the top and fended off the offers of life support, the views across the Meuse and the city were really quite something, and I'm not at all surprised the *Huffington Post* once placed the attraction at number one in its list of most extreme stairways (there seems to be a list or a day for everything these days). Once I'd recovered, I headed back down and waited for the terminal leg wobble to subside, before climbing on a bus back to the station. Struggling off the bus at Guillemins, I realised that the jelly legs were clearly going to take their time, and to be honest, I'm not entirely sure they've ever been right since...

Train travel thoughts D

If you're a solo female traveller, be aware that women-only couchettes are an option on most overnight trains these days.

Make sure you always fully acquaint yourself with route options; there's often an alternative, and it may be cheaper and/or more scenic.

Always check how far the main station is from the city centre – and get a taxi or a bus if it's a long way and you're planning to spend most of the day on foot/going up and down 800 steps.

E

E1 - Elsinore to Amsterdam – on the North West Express (Nord West Express)

Route: Elsinore – Copenhagen – Rødby – Puttgarden – Lübeck – Hamburg – Bremen – Osnabrück – Bad Bentheim – Hengelo – Amersfoort - Amsterdam

The prospect of some journeys fills us with more excitement than others, and for me, this was one of those trips. I'm not entirely sure why... but the name of the train alone was enough to make me briefly feel like an interesting character in a James Bond novel or a Hitchcock film. I'd spent a couple of days in Malmö, Sweden, and was now heading to Holland. At this point in the mid-1980s, the famous Öresund Bridge was still just an idea, so getting to Denmark meant taking a train up the coast to the Swedish port of Helsingborg and then catching the ferry for the short twenty-minute hop to Elsinore (Helsingør in Danish). The only thing I knew about Elsinore was that it was where Shakespeare's Hamlet was set. And sure enough, arriving on the ferry from Sweden offers a fantastic view of Kronborg Castle. Somehow this just added to the sense of excitement for me – marking the start of the journey on a note of historical and literary significance. Elsinore's railway station is right by the ferry terminal so it couldn't have been easier. And in no time at all, there I was standing in front of the Nord West Express! This train, sadly another casualty of the great 90s cull, was once a regular nightly connection between Scandinavia and Holland. In the summer months there were often direct through coaches from Stockholm to Amsterdam and the Hook of Holland for passengers travelling onwards to Harwich and the UK. On the evening of my departure, the train started from Elsinore, so travellers from Sweden and Norway also made the ferry crossing from Helsingborg. For many years, an alternative daytime service operated under the name of the Scandinavia Holland Express (and vice versa - see U below for more on this train).

As a student at the time, I was trying my best to eke out my limited budget by travelling overnight in seated compartments. This was a double saving as it avoided the couchette supplement and a night in a hostel or hotel. The carriage I got into was a German one, and anyone in the know with any sense would have done the same. This was because German carriages on night trains often had seats which you could pull out and make into a sort of couchette berth by doing the same with the seat opposite – providing of course there was nobody already sitting in it. Amazingly, I found myself once again the sole occupant of the compartment. Looking back now, and reflecting on what I said above about the Duisburg to Munich train, I'm starting to wonder whether I had a major BO issue I was totally unaware of, or was it just that there really were fewer folks travelling? Again, I suppose I'll never know, but either way, it was lovely having the compartment to myself. Given the number of intermediate stops in cities where people boarded the train, this is even more surprising. In this case, I think the timing may have been crucial. Although it was summer, it was late August by this point, a time when many young Europeans are back at school and university – and as such, a comfortable time for lone travellers like me who appreciate a bit of space.

In less than an hour, the train pulled into Copenhagen. Despite what looked like lots of activity outside on the platform, I still managed to keep the compartment for myself (I'm leaning more towards the BO theory). This was especially pleasing because I knew that the next major city where people were likely to board in any numbers was Hamburg, a good five or more hours away, meaning I could be fairly confident of some undisturbed kip in the meantime. Tired as I was though, I actually wanted to stay awake to see exactly what happened when the train got to Rødby. I'd read that this is where the carriages were individually shunted onto the ferry and clamped down for the crossing to Puttgarden on the German island of Fehmarn, before heading south to Hamburg. This was something I'd never experienced and it seemed like an intriguing operation to stay awake for. But what happened? Well, you've guessed it – I nodded off, and the next thing I remember was stirring when there was a ticket inspection in Hamburg. I'd slept through the whole thing - unbelievable. Particularly so as my older self now wakes up at the drop of a hat, so Lord knows how I'd managed to sleep through mass shunting in the Baltic (ooh missus). So I look back on this in both amazement and regret, especially as this route ceased to operate in 2019. Trains between Hamburg and Copenhagen now head up to Kolding on Jutland, before crossing via bridge to the Danish island of Funen, and then across the Great Belt Bridge to Zealand and Copenhagen. It's a bit longer in mileage terms (the old route was in fact called the 'As the Crow Flies Line' – Vogelfluglinie), but faster by about twenty minutes.

After Hamburg, I slumbered on as the train headed westwards through northern Germany and on into Holland. From a scenic point-of-view, this is one journey that is best done at night, unless endless flat fields are your thing. Nearly thirteen hours after leaving Elsinore, the train pulled into the great iron arches of Amsterdam Central Station at around 10.00, where it could rest till the evening before doing the return journey northwards. As mentioned, the North West Express managed to survive with some changes until the mid-1990s, after which there was no direct connection between the Dutch and Danish capitals until CNL introduced the Borealis service in 2006 - which sadly ceased in 2014.

E2 - Eskişehir to Istanbul – on a Turkish high-speed train

Route: Eskişehir – Bozüyük – Bilecik – Arifiye – Izmit –

Gebze – Pendik – Bostanci – Söğütlüçeşme (Istanbul)

This was a very welcome return rail journey to Istanbul after a somewhat trying road trip in the reverse direction on arrival in the country. I'd travelled to Turkey with two work colleagues for a week of project meetings in the Anatolian city of Eskişehir, situated roughly half way between Istanbul and Ankara. Access from Ankara would have been easier, but as there were no direct flights from Birmingham, flying to Istanbul was the next best option. We'd hoped to be able to get the last train of the day from Istanbul, but unfortunately, this departed quite soon after our flight arrived in the early evening. One of my colleagues (who'd visited Turkey on several occasions) assured us he could get a friend to pick us up at the airport and drive us the 300 km to Eskişehir. This seemed like an amazing offer – but as we know, things sometimes really are too good to be true.

When we finally managed to get out of Istanbul's immense airport, the first task was to try and locate my colleague's friend. By this point, he hadn't received a reply to any of his texts but we were hopeful something would come through before too long. After an unsettling silence, a message was finally received - his friend was waiting in a nearby car park. When we got to it, it was pretty huge as car parks go; 'What sort of car does your friend have, and what does he look like?' we asked. It turned out he didn't know. He wasn't actually a friend; he was a follower on Twitter and he'd never met him before. This wasn't filling me with confidence.

After quite a while spent scouring the car park with the eagerness of novice doggers, we eventually spotted someone waving – someone who looked like Doc Brown from the *Back to the Future* films. My colleague seemed satisfied that this was 'our man', so the three of us tried to get into the car. I say tried because it was full of all sorts of stuff – bags, shopping, junk. Even the boot was crammed – clearly, prior communications had not made things very clear. Not at all surprisingly since we soon discovered that Turkish Doc Brown couldn't speak a word of English, and sadly, none of us spoke any Turkish. I can only assume that Google translate had been used pre-arrival. So there we were, wedged in, cases on laps on a wet Monday night in January, and just a short 300 km drive ahead of us.

Istanbul airport is west of the city, so heading east meant we had to cross the entire metropolis of sixteen million people; the challenge of leaving European Turkey was added to by the bottleneck effect of having to cross one of the few bridges that span the Bosporus. So after two hours of driving and queuing, we still hadn't even left Istanbul. Eventually, the urban sprawl thinned out and we were travelling through dark mountainous terrain. This must have been incredibly scenic by day, but as it got later and later, it all just felt unsettling, especially when it started snowing. I think we all nodded off a little, including the driver himself at one point, as we came to a terrifying, screeching halt at a set of traffic lights, seemingly in the middle of nowhere. The breaks had been slammed on so hard that some damage had clearly been done – I'm talking smoke churning up from under the bonnet and an engine that refused to restart.

So there we were – broken down, in what was the middle of the night by now, in the remote Turkish mountains, and not exactly suitably attired. And it's January, and snowing. We got out of the car, as without lights in the darkness we were in danger of being hit by another vehicle. Doc Brown made a lengthy and what sounded like quite fraught call on his mobile – we hoped it was to the Turkish RAC or equivalent. I've had some weird nights in my life, and this one is certainly up there on the list. After an hour or two, a tow truck arrived and our spirits lifted - slightly. We piled into the truck and hoped we'd be taken on to our hotel in Eskişehir. But it transpired we were being driven to a workshop for the necessary repairs to be undertaken. On the one hand, we were incredibly impressed that mechanics were prepared to crack on with this at 3.00 in the morning – not sure that'd be the case in the UK. On the other hand, we were cold, very tired and just wanted to get some sleep before our first meeting at 9.00. Eventually, we managed to make ourselves understood, and one of the mechanics generously offered to drive us to our hotel where we finally checked in at just gone 5.00. We'd landed at Istanbul at around 18.00 the evening before – I'll say no more.

The following days were fortunately less traumatic; project meetings were held and work stuff got done. Before long it was time to look into the return journey and the good news was that we could get an early morning high-speed train to Istanbul that would give us enough time to get to the airport. So on Saturday morning we made our way to the railway station. I was surprised by the heavy security presence, and our cases and bags were scanned airport-style on entry to the building – a sad reflection on the current state of the world. Once through, we headed to the platform. Looking up and seeing the indicator displaying 'ISTANBUL' was thrilling, though glancing around at that early hour, the excitement seemed to be lost on everyone else. Businessmen casually flicked through newspapers, parents corralled their children, a group of women dressed in black burkas chatted animatedly. And, soon enough, the train pulled in.

And I have to say – what a train. Sleek and modern design, comfortable, spacious, panoramic windows, WiFi, onboard service, electronic displays showing train speed (the top speed was 250 km/h) and our current position on a digital map of Turkey. This was nothing like the Bosporus Express (see section I - Istanbul to Bucharest below) that I'd travelled on some years before. This was a 21st Century train built for a discerning public who didn't expect to have to pay the earth for the privilege either. And though the struggles concerning HS2 have been a hugely divisive issue in the UK, it's hard not to make unfavourable comparisons with the obvious progress that has clearly been made in Turkey. High-speed trains currently operate on six routes in the country, and there are already plans for further extensions and developments. As such, super-fast trains will soon be running all the way from the country's border with Bulgaria to the Syrian frontier. Maybe one day we'll manage Old Oak Common to Birmingham... no doubt for the price of a fortnight in Spain. Nuff said.

As the train pulled out, I glanced at the illuminated Eskişehir platform sign for the last time. It was strange to think that passengers would have once travelled through this very station on their way from Istanbul to far-flung destinations like Baghdad and Tehran at a similarly unearthly hour. Who knows, they might also have looked out of the window and seen the same sign – thousands of disparate lives connected perhaps only briefly over the decades by this one tiny point of commonality. For a city that's not exactly a household name (outside of Turkey), I was also surprised to see how vast the railway complex surrounding the station was. I later learned that the city is home to the largest railway and locomotive factory in the country – mystery solved.

By the time it got light, we started to see some of the amazing rugged scenery we'd travelled through in darkness on the way there – snow-capped mountains and exotic barren rock-scapes that looked other-worldly and stretched on almost endlessly. This was a fantastic experience, and appreciated all the more by contrast with the outward journey. Sitting back and relaxing in comfort and style, watching the extraordinary scenery go by with a coffee and breakfast – it was such a shame we'd missed that last train on the way there. But at least it left us with a tale to tell. The only slight issue was that, because of construction work, the train terminated at the pronunciation challenge that is Söğütlüçeşme – a busy suburban station on the Asian side of Istanbul. It would have been nice to have had time to get a ferry across the Bosporus and take in the wonderful city skyline, but as it was, there was only time to jump in a taxi and get across to the airport. These days, trains link the Asian part of Istanbul with Europe via the 14 km Marmaray Tunnel, the deepest undersea railway tunnel in the world. Though it was always more a collection of connecting services than a through train, it's an exciting thought that one day (if the world can ever sort itself out...), the magical Taurus Express of the 1930s could thus be reborn and run all the way from London to Baghdad and Aleppo. Who knows, it might even have a high-speed through coach for Birmingham...

Train travel thoughts E

Think carefully about when you travel – if you're able to travel out of the local peak season, it can make for a slightly quieter/more pleasurable experience.

Be wary of accepting lifts from strangers, however old you are.

Be wary of friends or colleagues arranging such lifts.

F

F1 - Fredericia to Hamburg – on the Northern Arrow (Nordpfeil/Nordpilen)

Route: Fredericia – Kolding – Vojens – Tinglev – Padborg – Flensburg – Schleswig – Neumünster - Hamburg

The Northern Arrow was once an important daytime connection between Hamburg in the north of Germany and the port of Frederikshavn, situated around 500 km further north towards the top of the Jutland peninsula in Denmark – a journey of around nine hours. Regular ferry services operate from the port to Oslo and Gothenburg, so the Northern Arrow (Nordpfeil in German, Nordpilen in Danish) used to be a good option for travellers heading to various destinations in Scandinavia, and for Scandinavians heading south into Germany and beyond. En route, it also stopped at Århus, Denmark's second largest city (see C3), and Ålborg, its fourth largest. The service originally began in 1936, and with the exception of short periods of suspension during the war, it ran until 1991. For the following ten years, it operated as a German InterRegio (IR) service that extended further south to Hanover and Göttingen. Between 1960 and 1983, a night train called the Kattegat Express ran on the same route. Up until the 1980s, an additional un-named daily express service ran backwards and forwards between Cologne and Frederikshavn, later truncated to Ålborg, then to Århus, and finally shortened even further to Fredericia.

I used both of these services fairly regularly in the 1980s, visiting Malene in Århus. The last time I travelled this way was in 2001, coming back from a visit to Northern Jutland. By this time, the Northern Arrow no longer covered the entire stretch, so heading south meant catching a local train from Ålborg to Fredericia. Fredericia always sounded like an exotic place to me, at least the way I pronounced it in my mind. (When pronounced correctly by a Dane, it sounds like they're releasing a meatball from the back of the throat.) Lying on the east coast of Jutland, it's a fairly small but not unattractive town, founded in the 17th Century by Frederick III (hence its name). There's an impressive white tower from the early 1900s which offers great views of the coast and over the Little Belt (which always sounds like a Hans Christian Andersen fairytale to me – it isn't). Its coastal position just at the edge of the Little Belt (still think he missed an opportunity there) makes it quite an important railway junction, as most Danish trains travelling north-south and east-west pass through and give the station the look and feel of belonging to a much bigger city. In fact, its position is of such strategic importance that, a few years ago, German Railways extended their overnight ski-train services northwards from Hamburg to Fredericia. This gave travellers from all over Denmark direct access to a whole range of popular destinations and winter resorts in the French and Swiss Alps, including Geneva, Albertville, Bourg St. Maurice and Montreux.

But my last visit to Fredericia was just a short stop at the station to pick up the IR Northern Arrow service down to Hamburg – an afternoon hop of just over three hours. This is by no means a dramatic or particularly grand journey but it is lovely – gentle views of woodland, rolling fields, heathland, coast and sea. On a sunny afternoon, it's the sort of trip that nourishes the soul. There's something refreshing about a journey like this, especially when the train isn't packed to the gunnels and you can relax, looking out of the window, comforted by peace and quiet inside and out. At some point, there will of course be somebody with a screaming baby from hell who comes and sits behind you (no offence to young – or old – parents/babies/demons) but you know what I mean. When did parents stop trying to placate screaming children? Is the thinking that they'll end up emotionally stunted if attempts are made to control them at an early age or something? Answers on a postcard please (but not to me).

The beauty of the first generation of German InterRegio services (1988 – 2003) was that, because you didn't need a reservation (or to pay a supplement), you could sit anywhere you liked, so you could always get up and look for a different seat (should a baby be exercising its lungs in your lugholes, for instance). Another great thing about the old IR services was their appearance. They'd been designed with great flair and style. The brand was built around various shades of blue plus white, and the IR carriages had a range of comfortable and swish compartment types. Many also had a dining car (the 'IR Bistro Cafe') where you could pass the time in some style. Once I'd escaped from decibel Damien, it was lovely having a Tuborg and a chat with Torben from Tinglev, even if he did bend my ear on Danish brewing techniques through the ages.

Before too long, it was immaterial anyway as the train pulled into its final destination, Hamburg Hauptbahnhof (the country's busiest railway station). For me, there's always something really exciting about arriving in Germany's northern metropolis and second city - the big city hustle and bustle, the glimpses of waterscapes offered by the River Elbe and the Alster, and its infamous Red Light reputation. There's something about a lot of port cities that injects them with that extra shot of dynamism. Hamburg might not have Munich's architectural flair or the romance of Heidelberg but it packs a punch when it comes to atmosphere and buzz, from the Reeperbahn and Grosse Freiheit area to the wonderful Speicherstadt (Warehouse district). In the past, the station itself was also a place of wonder (for me at least), with direct trains departing for destinations right across Europe, from Spain and Yugoslavia to Norway and Hungary. Waiting for a train back to the Hook of Holland or Ostend as a student, I'd often marvel at the sight of the night train to Oslo or Milan – services now long since gone, just like the Northern Arrow.

Today, unnamed Danish services still trundle back and forth between Hamburg and Fredericia, where you can alight to pick up trains heading further north. And with a couple more changes (and five hours to spare), it's still possible to get up to Frederikshavn and even to Skagen (40 km further on), the northernmost town in Denmark, where the North Sea and the Baltic magically meet. Skagen is incidentally home to Scandinavia's only teddy bear museum (who'd have thought?)... decibel Damien warning!

F2 - Freiburg (im Breisgau) to Basle – on D 483 – the night train from Copenhagen

Route: Freiburg – Basle Bad Bf – Basle SBB

This was a short day trip from the Black Forest to Switzerland in around 1990 when Margaret and I were staying in a small village just outside the medieval city of Freiburg. Freiburg itself has to be one of Germany's most attractive destinations. For a start, its location is hard to beat, perched as it is just on the edge of the Black Forest and almost completely surrounded by lovely mountain views. The old town is full of quirky old buildings, many of which date back hundreds of years – Martin's Tower, the Swabian Tower, its impressive cathedral, the Augustinian Museum - and there are wonderful views of them all from the Schlossberg (castle hill). Weirdly, one of the things that most impressed me is its unusual system of open gutters (I can hear pages being turned over). I know that doesn't ordinarily sound like anything most people would want to see, but these 13th Century water channels permeating the centre add a great deal of charm to the streets, a bit like Hobson's Conduit on Trumpington Street in Cambridge. They were apparently built to provide a water supply for farm animals and fighting fires.

But let me move on from medieval gutters and the various splendours of Freiburg. After this, and several days of hiking and scenic overload in the Black Forest, I fancied a train trip down to Basle in Switzerland. The two cities are well connected by rail, with several trains an hour, each taking roughly an hour. For quite some time now, high-speed German ICE trains have also connected the two places. But back in 1990, I didn't want to jump on any old regional or fast train – I wanted to travel down on the then fairly recently re-introduced night train from Copenhagen to Basle. An additional aim was seeing if I could get hold of the train destination sign (tick), and having a look at the various carriages (second tick). I know that sounds like a weird mixture of trainspotting and train porn, and maybe it is, but I can't deny the sense of excitement I feel walking through a long-distance night train, even if I'm only on it for an hour.

Dwelling for a moment on the train route, Copenhagen to Basle had been a staple night connection between northern and central Europe for many years. A journey of around fifteen to sixteen hours, several direct trains travelled in both directions until recent years. In various periods, these included the Basel/Italia/Schweiz Express, the unnamed D 483, and most recently, the CNL Aurora service which ceased operation in 2016. Since then, there has been no direct connection but with fast trains in both directions to and from Hamburg, travelling between Denmark and Switzerland is still very straightforward. This last 70 km section of the route is easily one of the most scenic as the train travels right the way through the Black Forest to Switzerland, with unspoilt picture postcard views of tiny villages huddling down in the hills and mountains, in between forests and rivers.

After admiring the scenery for a while, I had a walk through the train. There was a mixture of Danish and German sleeping cars and couchette coaches, alongside seating compartments that had probably been added on in Hamburg or Frankfurt. Glancing through the compartment windows, I noticed the usual array of bulging rucksacks, half-eaten snacks and ruffled bedding, all telling tales of the night just gone. As I stood at the end of one of the carriages (contemplating 'acquiring' an additional sign), I remember I was joined by someone I took to be a German businessman (looking far too smart and fresh for that time of day). He lit up a cigarette and just stood there staring at me - peculiar. I wasn't sure whether I was getting the glad eye or an imminent black eye... Slightly irked and bemused, I returned the stare without speaking (never wise to get into the 'what you looking at mate' game). This didn't deter him, so I just shambled off – always the best policy.

Minutes later, we pulled into Basle, Switzerland's third largest city, just on the border with Germany and France. This makes it a very important rail hub, a fact which is reflected in its unique distinction of having three main railway stations, each run by different European networks – Basle SBB (Switzerland); Basel Badischer Bahnhof (Germany) and Bâle SNCF (France). At this time in the late 1980s/early 1990s, Basle was still the best connected city in Switzerland, with direct trains running to destinations all over the Continent from Spain to Russia.

I got off at the railway immensity that is SBB station, from where it's just a short stroll into the old city centre where you can cross the various bridges spanning the Rhine; for my money, the medieval Mittlere Brücke is arguably the most attractive. Basle is apparently widely regarded as Switzerland's cultural centre, with its large number of museums, galleries and the country's oldest university. At different points in its history, it was also home to such noted intellectuals as Erasmus, Jung and Nietzsche. But I have to confess that my main priority was a bit more low-brow - a trip to the train depot to make enquiries about train signs, where, I'm pleased to report, they were very helpful. After that, I spent a very pleasant afternoon looking round the city and enjoying an over-priced beer or two.

When I got back to the station, I still had a fair bit of time before catching the train back to Freiburg, so I decided to have a walk along some of the platforms (sometimes you just have to own your nerdiness). As mentioned, the range of direct destinations from Basle at the time was staggering. I was delighted to see the Geneva-Moscow train coming in on the platform I was standing at. The Soviet coaches were fascinating – they looked incredibly austere with their dowdy green livery that made them look like they'd been converted from old military tanks (maybe they had). I stood peering in through a filthy window with faded little orange curtains pulled to the side, only to jump out of my skin when an angry finger tapped violently at the window, no doubt resentful of my staring (guilty as charged, your honour). The windows were so dirty, it had been impossible to see if anyone was actually in the compartment. I did wonder whether there might be a way of removing the wonderful destination sign from the side of the carriage, but thought that might provoke more angry finger tapping, or worse still, a night in a Swiss jail, so it went no further - unlike the train, which would still take another two days to reach Moscow at a snail's pace. I waved to the invisible tapper(s) and made my way back to the Freiburg train, glad it would only be an hour or so before I was tucking into some wholesome Black Forest fare back in the hotel.

Train travel thoughts F

Avoid sitting near babies if you can – they're bound to start screaming at some point.

In cities with several stations, make sure to check which is the best one for the city centre.

Whether intentionally or unintentionally, don't stare at Russians or German businessmen (or anyone really) through train windows or otherwise.

G

G1 - Geneva to Venice – on the Simplon Express

Route: Geneva – Lausanne – Brig - Domodossola – Milan – Verona - Venice

If Freiburg to Basle doesn't sound like a particularly romantic or glamorous journey, Geneva to Venice certainly does, to me at least. Especially when it's a journey on the Simplon Express – again, not to be confused with its luxury near-namesake, the Venice Simplon Orient Express, though it did follow much of the same route, and owes its name to the old Simplon Orient Express that ran for many years between Paris and Istanbul after the end of the First World War. Re-introduced in 1962, the starting-point of the Simplon Express was Paris, from where the 2000 km two-night journey across Europe to Belgrade began. Travelling south through France from the Gare de Lyon, the train passed through the Simplon Tunnel in Switzerland before dipping down towards Milan, across to Venice and Trieste, then heading south into the former Yugoslavia. And so it continued for the next thirty years or so until the outbreak of the Balkan War in the early 1990s when the destination was initially shortened to Vinkovci on the Croatian-Serbian border. As the war progressed, this was further truncated to Zagreb, then Ljubljana, and eventually to Trieste. In 1992, the service from Paris came to an end, partly because a new and faster TGV connection served the stretch between Paris and Lausanne. Its new departure point then became Geneva, and Zagreb the new destination, though this was extended south again to Vinkovci in 1997; by 2000, it had been re-shortened to Trieste, and in 2001, the service was finally - and sadly - withdrawn altogether, ending a significant chapter in international railway history.

My journey on the Simplon Express was late 1990s, so by this time I was boarding the train at its departure point in Geneva. I'd booked a berth in a six-couchette compartment (yet again – why don't I learn?) and soon realised with some disappointment that the compartment was fully occupied, and I was the last one to enter. This made for a slightly awkward and unrelaxed start to the journey, as we all shuffled about, struggling to store our luggage at the same time. As it was summer, it was also hot... very hot, and the air-conditioning appeared to be on the blink. So from the get-go it was clear this was going to be a warm one. Add to the mix some Balkan bruiser who had obviously decided deodorant was for wimps, and you have that winning heat-stink combo that is the perfect finishing touch on any ten-hour overnight journey. Breathe in and weep. This was entirely my own fault of course for having been too mean to book a sleeping compartment – a lesson I have repeatedly failed to learn. After a while though, when everyone had settled down and my nostrils had adjusted, it didn't seem too bad. That said, I remember lying on my bunk wondering how this compared to travelling on the train in the glamorous, heady days of the old Venice Simplon Express, just when the Balkan bruiser broke wind with unselfconscious pride. Maybe 'twas ever thus.

After a short corridor walk to see if there was a restaurant car (there wasn't), I bought a beer from the Croatian carriage attendant and retired to the sweatbox for the night. Barring the heat and assorted odours, the rest of the journey was fairly uneventful, even if – predictably – it wasn't the greatest ever night's sleep. Uneventful till Milan, that is, in the small hours of the next morning. It's never a surprise to hear a bit of hustle and bustle going on when a train arrives in a major city, as people jostle to get off or on. But suddenly, whatever was going on further down the carriage was a lot more than this. In fact, it was quite a commotion – shouting, banging, screaming. Everyone in the compartment was immediately awake and on their guard, the overhead light was flicked on, and the Balkan bruiser rushed out to see what was happening.

Word soon spread that a thief had boarded the train and been caught rifling through somebody's valuables. The passengers who'd caught him had decided to vent their anger and indignation by beating him up. The shouting and piercing screams that accompanied the fracas were truly horrendous, and I don't think I was the only one relieved when the railway police intervened. After some time, we were finally on our way again – tired and rather unsettled. As mentioned, I'd heard of these kinds of incidents before – people had often warned me about certain trains in different countries, and over the years, fellow passengers had shared railway horror stories of all sorts. I sometimes wondered how true they were, or to what extent they were embroidered with each retelling. I remember a time in the 1980s when there were tales of masked robbers boarding night trains in France and pouring chloroform into air-conditioning systems so that the people they robbed were suitably comatose by the time their valuables disappeared. How true they were, I've never been able to establish. I also remember a Bulgarian colleague warning me about travelling overnight through Romania – gypsy gangs would hijack entire trains and ransack passengers' belongings. Again, I've never been inclined to believe such stories, but hearing all the commotion that morning in Milan, it did confirm that vigilance is always the best policy. And more recently, tales abound of travellers having their cases stolen from the 'communal' luggage racks at the end of train carriages – scary.

I spent the next couple of hours catnapping until the train arrived in Venice, my first ever visit to the city, and what a wonderful time to arrive, 6.30 on a Sunday morning. The massive concrete block that is Venice Santa Lucia station was not really what I was expecting for a city synonymous with romance and glamour, but you're soon out of it (and it does have a sort of brutal minimalist charm from outside). As soon as you walk outside, there is absolutely no mistaking where you are – there it is, Venice, in all its enchanting glory. I've often found that many 'famous' places fall short of our expectations when we actually visit them. For me, Venice is not one of those, and seeing it for the first time at what must surely be the best time of the week – an early summer Sunday morning, still practically deserted, the hordes of day tourists not yet arrived or up and about, it really felt like having a private walk around a Canaletto painting.

During the daytime, as everyone knows, it's a different matter. The massive numbers of tourists that descend (all bemoaning each other) do slightly detract from everyone's ideal 'Venetian experience', but you don't always have to wander too far from the main tourist spots to reclaim some peace and quiet. But even with the heaving masses and the tourist kitsch, it's still just wonderful. I especially love wandering about at night when it's much quieter again. And – as someone (like many of my generation) who saw the film *Don't Look Now* at an impressionable age – you can't help looking out for that little red figure disappearing over a canal bridge into a sottoportego. I'm surprised nobody (to my knowledge) has ever decided to don a red duffel coat as a prank and run around the Venetian alleyways at night. That could certainly be one way to shrink the numbers of tourists there, though thinking about it, inducing heart attacks might not be the best way to go about it.

G2 - Groningen to Leer – on the regional D 933

Route: Groningen – Winschoten – Nieuweschans – Weener – Leer

This train trip was a relatively short cross-border run that followed a fairly gruelling journey up to Groningen in the northern Netherlands. I was heading up to Germany to stay with my friend Ulrich whom I'd met on the school German exchange. He and his family lived just over the Dutch border in Ostfriesland (East Frisia). Still a 6th former at the time, money was fairly tight despite the small fortune I was (not) earning in my two Saturday jobs – one on the early morning shift at the local bakery inserting jam into donuts, and the other as a dance hall cloakroom attendant at the opposite end of the day. The tales I could tell after all those Saturday nights sitting there with my book of raffle tickets and tin of pins...another time.

To cut down on expense, the plan was to hitchhike across the Midlands to Harwich, get the ferry to Holland and then hitch north to Groningen to pick up the train to Leer in Germany. I was delighted to get an early morning lift from home to the outskirts of Birmingham, and even more delighted when a lorry driver heading straight for Harwich picked me up shortly after that. Although I have absolutely no memory of what we talked about, I do vividly remember we chatted all the way to the coast. This amazes me now. I'm not sure whether it's a post-

Covid/lockdown thing or just the effects of getting older, but the thought of hours of confined chat with a total stranger horrifies me now (socially phobic curmudgeon that I have become – apologies).

On the positive side, the time flew by and we arrived in Harwich in plenty of time for the day crossing to the Hook. Once on the ferry, I caught up on a bit of sleep and had a slow walk round the lorry-drivers' lounge, displaying my self-made Groningen hitching sign. I'd done this a few times before and it always made me feel a bit uncomfortable – it felt like an uneasy combination of begging and rough dating. Unfortunately, nobody seemed to be heading to northern Holland (or liked the look of me), so my spirits were starting to sink a little. After a few more slow walk-rounds, a Dutch lorry driver said he could drop me off by the motorway outside Rotterdam where I'd probably have a better chance of getting a lift. This looked as if it was going to be my only offer, so I gratefully accepted it.

Before too much longer, I was on the side of the road, sign fully extended and hopes on the high side. For a time, at least. After an hour of waiting, panic started to set in, especially as it was getting dark and chances of a lift were dwindling. After a further hour, a car pulled up offering a lift as far as Utrecht. This would get me a fair way further along, and I was certainly ready to sit down, so in I got. After an hour or so, I was dropped off again, and it was back to the same routine. Except that this time, it was really dark, I was very tired and seemingly in the middle of nowhere, surrounded by motorway sprawl. After a couple of hours I thought about walking off to try and find a hostel or somewhere to spend the night, but 1) I had no idea where I was exactly and it could have taken me hours of trudging to find something affordable; 2) there was always a chance that any minute I could get a lift. So I carried on waiting and hoping. After a few more hours, fortune finally smiled on me and I climbed into a lorry heading for Groningen.

The lorry driver dropped me off in the city centre at around 6.00 the next morning and pointed me towards the station. At that time of day, the last thing I wanted to do was explore Groningen. I've been a few times since and have to say it's a really lovely and somewhat underrated Hanseatic city. It's often described as the capital of the northern Netherlands, and although it's not as large or impressive as Amsterdam or Utrecht, it's a charming place to spend a day or so.

There was a train shortly after 7.00 heading for Germany, so I quickly bought my ticket and headed to the platform. D 933 was already waiting – it was such a relief to know I was finally on the last leg (and not just my last legs). Seeing it standing there felt like finding the Holy Grail – after a drawn-out and challenging slog getting there, it was like seeing an old, reliable friend who'd come to pick me up. That wonderful certainty of knowing the journey would soon be over. It wasn't very busy so I was happy to put my feet up on the seat opposite (shoes removed) and grab a snooze in what felt like blissful luxury. Opening my eyes between snoozes, the early morning scenery passed by – green fields, geometrically arranged and as flat as if God had been out with his Celestial iron for a damn good session. And here and there a distant windmill, just in case you needed reminding you were in Holland; it all felt incredibly peaceful and comforting. The scenery on both sides of the border this far up is in fact exactly the same, and even the German they speak in East Frisia - Plattdeutsch or Low German - is closer to Dutch in many respects.

The train had started from Groningen and was heading due east out of the Netherlands towards the country's northernmost border crossing with Germany at Nieuweschans, after which it would head on to the Low Saxon cities of Oldenburg, Bremen and Hanover, a total journey of about four hours. I'd managed to phone Ulrich before he left for college in the town of Leer. He offered to pick me up at the station but the thought of sitting in on his lessons for the morning wasn't exactly very appealing, even allowing for the reserves we can pull on at that age. So we agreed to meet at lunchtime and I spent the morning looking round the town. I'd been there a few times before on a previous visit and loved it – my first proper forays into Euro-discos and afternoon ice cream parlours (yes, I really was that much of an envelope-pushing teenage thrill seeker). To the adolescent me, Leer felt like an exotic and exciting destination; it was incredibly picturesque too, with its beautiful Renaissance town hall perched at the head of the little harbour. Watching the boats coming and going that morning was as nourishing as a few hours' sleep. I felt so intrepid and grown-up – I suppose it's that odd thing as an older teenager when you remember that only a couple of years previously you weren't allowed out after 21.00; and suddenly you've matured into a world explorer (well... you've travelled overnight through Holland and got to Germany but as we know, it's not all about size/distance).

These days, there are still regular trains from Groningen to Germany but they all stop at the German border town of Weener for onward bus and rail connections to Leer and beyond. I've not been back to the town since those days but would very much like to; that said, I think it'd probably be quite a poignant return, having last been there at a point in life when everything was ahead of me and still to play for... and now as a maudlin git approaching the end of the game (hopefully with a good chunk of extra time too). And yes, my cheery disposition is legendary.

Train travel thoughts G

There's rarely a need to be paranoid on overnight trains but vigilance will always pay off; and lock the compartment door if you can.

Using a small chain to lock your suitcase to a distant luggage rack can save a lot of grief – always favour the nearby overhead ones if they're big enough.

A bit of vapour rub under your nose is often a good way to mask any compartment odours someone might generously be sharing.

Early mornings are often the best times for sightseeing and taking photos, even if like me you're not a natural early riser.

Try not to turn into a maudlin old fart, and if you do, don't go on about it (apologies).

H

H1 - Heidelberg to Ostend – on the Tauern Express

Route: Heidelberg – Mannheim – Mainz – Bonn – Cologne – Aachen – Liège – Brussels – Ghent – Bruges - Ostend

My first time on the Tauern Express was in 1983. After my A levels, I took a gap year (or a year out as we used to call it in those days) before going to university. I spent the first part of that year working as an English teaching assistant at a school just outside the south-western German city of Heidelberg. Heidelberg is a charming medieval city that doesn't disappoint the tourist – wooded hills rising up from the banks of the Neckar River, ancient hill-top castle (it's said that Goethe used to wander around the park that surrounds it), picturesque half-timbered buildings, and so on. The old town is lovely and I spent many a happy afternoon walking along the Philosophenweg (Philosophers' Way) near the Heiligenberg, from where the views are breathtaking. In short, it's well worth a visit, and I felt extremely lucky having the opportunity to spend five or so months in the area - all the more so for having grown up in a small Midlands town that didn't exactly wear its charms on its sleeve. As far as my eighteen-year-old self was concerned, I was living life and loving it.

I began working at the school at the start of the school

year in September, and as is always the case, the end of term Christmas holidays soon rolled round. The most direct way back home to the Midlands was to get up to Ostend to catch the Dover ferry, before carrying on up to Birmingham and home. Fortunately, there was a direct daily train from Heidelberg to Ostend. Unfortunately, it left at 1.26 in the morning and, understandably, nobody was willing to sacrifice their night's sleep to get me to the station just in time for the train. So at the end of the school day (which was early afternoon in German schools in those days), I made my way into the city, stored my case in a luggage locker, and tried to entertain myself for the rest of the afternoon, evening and night. I don't know what it is, but when you know you're essentially killing time for hours at a stretch, it's very difficult to just relax and enjoy the passing time.

There's something about watching the clock and constantly monitoring how much time is left before your train leaves. A bite to eat and a few beers is never a bad way to start of course, and the cinema seemed another good option. After all, it was a bitterly cold December evening, and a few hours in the warmth was more than welcome. What was the only film showing? *Jaws 3* – in 3D. I absolutely loved *Jaws* so this seemed a great idea. I'll refrain from going the full Barry Norman on *J3D*, as I think enough has probably been said about it, but it was at least a warm refuge for a few hours. After leaving the cinema, the inevitable point finally arrived – there were still a couple of hours to kill but I'd had enough of wandering around and stretching out beers, so it was time to wait it out at the station.

In the 1980s, I seemed to spend quite a lot of time on various European stations waiting for connections at night and, I can tell you, it was always grim. I'm sure somebody has carried out sociological research into the demographic dynamics of yesteryear railway stations at night. I haven't, but for what they're worth, my conclusions are that they were a refuge for the marginal – the homeless, beggars, sex workers, people with psychological issues who'd perhaps slipped through the system... and of course, tired travellers like me who felt like they'd drifted into a tortured Soft Cell song. By day, stations were full of the busy and the beautiful, heading off hither and thither for business or pleasure. By night, those on the fringes reclaimed the space. These days, stations tend to close at night or if not, access is much more tightly controlled, no doubt due to security concerns. This is, of course, totally understandable but I have to confess to feeling strangely rather nostalgic about those night-time railway grimscapes.

Soon enough it was time to head down to the platform and wait for the train to come in. And what a sight it was – the Tauern Express, pulling in with a mixture of carriages owned by Yugoslav, German, Belgian and Austrian Railways. The service was first introduced in 1951, when it ran between Ostend and Ljubljana. In 1953, this was extended to Belgrade and, for a number of years in the later 1950s and early 1960s, there were even through coaches attached that covered the roughly 3000 km between Ostend and Athens – at that time, the longest continuous railway service in Europe. Over the years there were slight modifications to the route, and direct through coaches to various other cities were added and removed. For many years, Split on the Croatian coast took over from Belgrade as the final destination; carriages from Klagenfurt and Graz in south-eastern Austria were also added, while other carriages were uncoupled in Cologne and elsewhere, heading up to Hamburg and Dortmund. This collection of through coaches made the train a long and colourful sight to behold, and the passengers were an equally varied bunch. From its earliest days, the train had been particularly popular with Yugoslavian guest workers in Germany who could travel back and forth without changing trains, to places like Ljubljana, Zagreb and Belgrade. Given Yugoslavia's appeal as a holiday destination, the train also proved popular with UK passengers making the relatively short hop from Dover. And then, of course, there were the Belgian, German and other European holiday-makers.

The train was named after the Tauern Mountains in Austria, through which it passed on its two-night journey between the Belgian coast and the Yugoslav capital (three nights when it went on to Athens!). The idea of a direct train connection between north-western Europe and the

Balkans came from an unlikely sounding source - a German theologian from Stuttgart called Richard Ottmar, who was also something of a train timetable expert and rail enthusiast. He had championed the idea for many years and is widely regarded as the father of the Tauern Express. Like so many other services, however, it was not to survive, and was eventually withdrawn in 1988. An unnamed shorter service survived for a few more years between Ostend and Salzburg, before it too finally disappeared from the timetables.

But back to that December night in 1983 – I was so happy to get on the train finally at 1.30 in the morning, for the eight hour journey up to Ostend. By day, this journey offers absolutely magnificent views of the Rhine, particularly around Koblenz, which I'd seen when travelling down on my way there. It was just as well, as there was nothing to see in the dark of night. Although the train had several couchette and sleeping coaches, my budget at 18 didn't stretch that far, so it was a question of looking for a quiet seating compartment, which I'm pleased to say I found. The only thing was, it was absolutely freezing. As so often seemed to be the case, there was clearly an issue with the heating system. And before too long, a young German woman bustled into the compartment, disturbing what I hoped was going to be a peaceful night. At that time of night, I just wanted to get my head down and try for some kip, but she was determined to converse. Why did I feel obliged to respond to small-talk into the small hours? Why didn't I find a diplomatic way of saying, "Sorry, don't take this the wrong way, but I'm trying to get some shut-eye? It is after all 3.00 in the morning." Why did I let my concern to be polite scupper a snooze? Looking back, I often despair at some of the relatively minor things I didn't seem able to handle, but maybe that's just the awkward transition from youth to adulthood. To be honest, I'm not entirely sure I've improved at all now. Whatever the case, my first night on the Tauern Express left me arriving in Ostend as a very cold and irritable Mr Grump. And that was even before the onward slog across the Channel and up to the Midlands....

H2 - Hilversum to Bruges – on the Benelux run-around

Route: Hilversum – Utrecht – Rotterdam – Antwerp – Ghent – Bruges

As everyone knows, the Netherlands and Belgium are close neighbours with strong social, cultural and linguistic ties. And yet for all that, there have never been very many direct train services connecting Dutch and Belgian towns – so never a direct service, say, from Groningen to Ghent, Arnhem to Liège, Ostend to Utrecht, etc. The major rail link has long been the regular hourly service between Amsterdam and Brussels that went by the name of the 'Benelux Train' for many years. Admittedly, this service did connect some of both countries' biggest centres – including Amsterdam, The Hague and Rotterdam in Holland, and Antwerp and Brussels in Belgium - and, given excellent rail connections within each country to these major cities, I suppose it's never really mattered that much. The only issue is that some inter-Benelux journeys inevitably involve multiple changes. And so it was, the time Margaret and I went for a weekend break to Bruges; a relatively short trip of about 200 km from where we were living in Hilversum, but one that took us on four different trains.

Like most towns in Holland, Hilversum is well plugged into the country's rail system. Situated between Amsterdam and Utrecht, there have always been good connections to both these and other cities. The town itself is a decent enough place but there's little of interest for tourists. It's long been Holland's radio and TV centre, with most of the country's networks based there. For people of a certain age (like me), it's still a familiar name from radio dials of yesteryear. It also still gets a mention at Eurovision when they move to the votes of the Dutch jury; and talking Eurovision, the town hosted the third ever Song Contest back in 1958. The song that coincidentally came third that year was one of the most famous non-winners ever – the Italian song *Nel Blu Dipinto di Blu*, better known as *Volare*. But be that as it may, we had a train to catch!

The first one was on the local train to Holland's major rail hub, Utrecht. I've always loved the Dutch word for a local train – a 'stoptrein' – a literal translation of which is unsurprisingly a 'stop train' – a perfect description for a train that does exactly that every few miles. For all that, it was just a short fifteen minute hop, and then it was grab the bags and off in search of the intercity south to Rotterdam. It was a Friday, and as is the case everywhere, a busy travel day. So much so that when we got on the train, there didn't appear to be any free seats. After ten minutes of awkward shuffling and shambling down the aisles, multiple apologies and 'excuse me's', we eventually found a couple of empty seats in one of the smoking carriages (remember them?). And there was no doubting it – every single person seemed to have a fag on the go the whole time. No disrespect to folk who enjoy a smoke, but the concentration effect of a closed carriage meant that by the time we got off at Rotterdam Central forty minutes later, it felt like we'd passively smoked the equivalent of a packet of twenty and we stank like a pair of kippers.

We soon found the next train to Antwerp, which fortunately wasn't anywhere near as busy, and before long we crossed into Belgium. Even before Schengen, border controls very rarely took place between Holland and Belgium, I think because of internal Benelux agreements. The most obvious indication you weren't in Holland any more was seeing the little red and white number plates on the passing cars instead of the black and gold ones with big NL stickers. There were other signs as well –

suddenly, the ordered neatness of the Netherlands felt as if it had just loosened its collar a bit and kicked off its shoes. Things looked slightly grubbier here and there, and a lick of paint wouldn't have gone amiss in quite a few places. Don't get me wrong – I absolutely loved this about Belgium. It always felt quite refreshing after the somewhat OCD orderliness of Holland. It could just be that having grown up in the English Midlands of the 1970s, a bit of grot here and there felt very much like being at home. However, arriving in Antwerp Central was a far grander affair. This is another railway station high up on my list of faves – it's like arriving in some magnificent cathedral, with its vast dome, huge entrance hall and immense arched windows. But don't just take my word for it – the American magazine *Newsweek* listed it as the fourth greatest railway station in the world a few years ago, and it has received many other accolades over the years. It's not surprising it's been used in quite a few TV programmes, including Agatha Christie's *Poirot*.

But lovely as it is, it was time to track down the last train of the day and get to Bruges. So it was off with the bags once more and on with the spot the right platform challenge. It's a roughly ninety minute run from Antwerp to Bruges, but a very pleasant one, watching the gentle fields of Flanders pass by, and looking out for Ghent's impressive castle en route. Arriving in Bruges station is nothing like Antwerp Central – its station was built in the modernist 'international style' so it has the look of a big block of concrete. I'm probably being a bit harsh, but it's not on my personal list. It's also a good walk from there into the centre of Bruges, as is often the case with medieval towns and cities. But Bruges itself is *absolutely* on my list of favourite places.

Anyone who's ever been, or seen the film *In Bruges* for that matter, knows how beautiful it is. It's often described as one of the 'Venices of the North' (a list which also includes Birmingham – just saying) with its beautiful network of canals (I wonder if the Belgians ever call Venice the Bruges of the south?). And it also has the distinction of being one of the best preserved medieval cities in Europe. Given its position on the Ostend to Brussels line, it used to be well served by all the old international trains that headed from the coast via the capital and on into Germany, Austria, Italy, and so on, but those direct connections have sadly now all gone. But despite that, it's still served by regular cross-Belgium connections. It was actually the first town I ever visited abroad, thanks to a five-day coach trip from primary school when I was nine (God bless those teachers!), and I can still remember the magically mesmerising impression it made on me. In fact, you might say it was my first holiday romance... though I have a feeling it might have also been my first taste of unrequited love.

Train travel thoughts H

If you find yourself in a quiet mood with a chatty fellow

traveller, don't feel bad about not engaging – you're unlikely to see them ever again (unless it's your wife or husband, etc) and you're perfectly entitled to say you'd like to just watch the scenery or have a nap.

Obvious I know, but if you're doing a journey that involves multiple changes, make sure to give yourself plenty of time at each station.

I

I - Istanbul to Bucharest - on the Bosfor Express

Route: Istanbul – Edirne – Kapikule – Svilengrad - Dimitrovgrad – Gorna Orjahovitsa – Ruse – Giurgiu - Bucharest

Travelling by train to Istanbul has always struck me as an exotic adventure. I'm sure my view on this has been influenced by Agatha Christie's *Murder on the Orient Express* and the various film versions I've seen on TV over the years. But travelling to Turkey really is something special. Technically, arriving from the Continent at Istanbul Sirkeci Station means you're still in what is officially classed as European Turkey (about 3% of the country) but, be that as it may, it does feel different – oriental, exciting, genuinely like crossing into another culture. Other people might experience this differently but, for me, it felt like stepping into the glamour and mystery of the Near East. This feeling was even more overwhelming the time I crossed the Bosporus to visit the other main Istanbul station, perched grandly on the opposite side of the water – Haydarpaşa. Looking up at the departure board there and seeing trains heading for Iran and Syria seemed like the height of exoticism, though sadly I never have managed to get to any of these destinations (yet).

Since a fire in 2010, Haydarpaşa has unfortunately been

out of action but this was once Turkey's busiest railway station. As well as services crossing the length and breadth of the country, the Taurus Express used to run via Syria to Baghdad in Iraq (a distance of over 2500 km), while the Trans Asia Express covered over 3000 km en route to Tehran. Services such as these once made Istanbul an extremely well-connected city. From Sirkeci Railway Station on the European side, a number of direct trains used to run to an equally impressive list of Continental destinations, often on a daily basis:

- The Direct Orient Express to Sofia, Belgrade, Venice, Milan, Lausanne and Paris
- The (Hellas) Istanbul Express to Salzburg, Munich and Dortmund
- The Bosphor Express to Hamburg (a short-lived service)
- The Balkan Express to Sofia, Belgrade, Budapest and Vienna
- The Transbalkan to Bucharest and Budapest
- The Dostluk Express to Thessaloniki
- Istanbul to Athens

Unfortunately, none of the above named services operate any longer though there are still direct trains to Bucharest (the Bosfor) and to Sofia (the Sofia-Istanbul Express). Sadly, Sirkeci Station is no longer the departure or arrival point either, this now being the town of Halkali, about 25 km west of Istanbul, where passengers need to join a local light-rail service into the city centre. This is a shame, not just because it's less convenient, but also because arriving at Sirkeci – a beautifully historic station in its own right, and the former home of the Simplon Orient Express – meant travelling through the wonderful Byzantine Walls of Theodosius on the approach, and marvellous glimpses of the Marmara Sea.

Our journey leaving Istanbul was on the Bosfor Express to Bucharest. At the time, it was a late evening departure from the city at around 23.00, so it was another one of those strange days where you're conscious of clock-watching the whole time. We'd stayed in a hotel in the historic Sultanahmet district, so it was only a short taxi ride back to Sirkeci station, next to the Golden Horn. Despite the manic traffic we got there in good time, giving me the chance to have a final wander round the station. The Orient Express sign still adorned the wall outside the restaurant on platform one. Though the station might have been a shadow of its 19th Century self, it still felt incredibly atmospheric in the romantic glow of the evening lights. It was hard not to wonder what it must have been like arriving here from Paris in those early days, and what a sight it must have all been - Western aristocrats mingling with the Muslim masses amidst all the coming and going of porters, guides and passengers. The reality of the scene, as we stood there that evening waiting for the train to arrive, was rather tame by comparison – the Bosfor Express was the only train due in, and people stood around waiting patiently and fairly quietly for it. The engine driver sounded the horn as it slowly pulled in, prompting the usual increase in animation as everyone picked up their luggage and moved up and down the platform trying to anticipate where their carriage would finally stop.

We'd booked a sleeping compartment for the two of us, so at least we knew we could relax in privacy when we got on. Andrei, the Romanian attendant, opened the carriage door and welcomed us on board with a friendly smile and greeting. This was a pleasant surprise as on many occasions in the past I've often felt as if I was a slightly inconvenient intrusion, forcing them to put down their crossword with three clues still to solve. He showed us to our compartment and said he'd be along shortly to offer us drinks and snacks. This trip was over twenty years ago now and, even though the sleeping car was far from the latest design, it wasn't at all bad. Two comfortable bunks, your own table, basin with running water and a door you can lock – what more can you ask for? (Well, your own loo and shower, I suppose, and I understand compartments with these facilities are available on this route nowadays). As we pulled out of Istanbul, I felt quite sad to leave – it really is a city that makes an impression. Apparently, I'm not the only one who thinks so – it is now officially the most visited city in the world, and there really is plenty to see – I could wax lyrical about the mighty Blue Mosque, the Hagia Sophia, the spice bazaars and markets, and all the various sights, smells and sounds that overwhelm your senses at times, but any guidebook will do a much better job than I could.

As the train trundled out, we were treated to the wondrous sight that is this illuminated mega-city by night – an endless chaotic mass of light, buildings, monuments, traffic and people. It soon picked up speed and was thundering along in no time. I remember feeling that thrill again – in the dark of the hot Turkish night, that sense of being a long way from home and loving it. I stood leaning out of the open window for quite a while, enjoying the hot breeze against my face, seeing silhouettes of mosques and minarets against the dusky orange night sky. The train eventually left the urban sprawl and entered the midnight blackness of the countryside. Andrei still hadn't appeared with the drinks offer, so I walked down to his compartment – he'd nodded off. I'd knocked his open door before I realised; he was profusely sorry and insisted on giving me a couple of free beers as part of his apology. He seemed quite keen to chat; I asked him how long he'd been working as a sleeping car attendant – twenty years. I imagined it must be quite an exciting life, getting to travel all over Europe with your job. His answer surprised me, though on reflection it seemed obvious: spending your nights awake in a small compartment and your days trying to sleep with the carriage parked up in railway sidings outside Budapest or Belgrade wasn't exactly a thrill, he said. And all of it a real challenge for family life.

At a more opportune point in the conversation, I steered things round to the signs I collect – yes, he could get me lots of them, no problem, please give me your email address. I emphasised I was happy to pay him for them. By this point, it was time to bed down and try for some sleep myself. As is probably clear by now, this has always been a bit of a challenge for me, as someone who struggles with insomnia even at home. To add to the challenge, the knowledge that we'd be having to get up in the small hours at the Turkish-Bulgarian border didn't make things any better. Still to this day, passengers have to get off the train at Kapikule, the last stop in Turkey, and queue up to have their passports stamped.

This all takes quite some time just when you least need it, but at least in this direction, you can leave your luggage on board (in the opposite direction, you can't). I felt a little uneasy about this so made sure all my valuables were tucked into in my money belt. It was a bit awkward with the Persian rug. Yet again, I realised how much my life has been influenced by films and television; as we stood in the queue for customs and passports, I inevitably thought of the film *Midnight Express*, and I can still hear the main character's heart beating out of his chest as he desperately tries to act casual at customs. I did the same but fortunately had an easier time of it than Billy Hayes did (admittedly, I didn't have a shed load of drugs sellotaped to my midriff, so I suppose that probably helped).

Once we were all done, Andrei welcomed us safely back on board and we were off into the Bulgarian night for the long northward journey to Romania, meaning we could at least try for some uninterrupted sleep now. As night trains go, the actual distance between Istanbul and Bucharest at about 950 km is not enormous, but with border stops and speed-limited tracks, this was a very long journey of about twenty-one hours, and that's even without the frequent delays. But at least we had our own space, and when you know it's a long haul, somehow your tolerance threshold improves. At home, I tend to get really angry if a two-hour journey takes three; but when a twenty-one hour journey takes twenty-four, it doesn't really seem to matter as much.

Eventually at Ruse (see R1 – Ruse to Varna), we caught glimpses of the Danube which forms much of the border between Bulgaria and Romania. Climbing steadily up to what seemed to be a huge height above the river, the train literally inched forward. I marvelled at how wide the Danube is at this stretch (about 2 km), as we looked down on wooded islands far below in the middle of the river. The speed limit apparently had to do with the state of the bridge, built by the Soviets in the 1950s. Crossing the bridge felt a bit like an old Alton Towers ride that had been designed for the nervous and elderly – and possibly mad. Soon enough, and with some relief, we arrived in Giurgiu, the first town in Romania, and from here it was a relatively short run up to the capital, and the hectic delights of the Gara de Nord station (see B1). We said a brief goodbye to Andrei before stepping down from the carriage, and I was surprised he responded with a hug. I never did hear anything from him but I have absolutely no doubt he was completely sincere at the time.

Train travel thoughts I

If there's a particular journey you have on your bucket list, don't put it off indefinitely – it may disappear before you do.

It never hurts to keep on the right side of a sleeping car attendant, especially if you're on a train that you'll need to get off temporarily.

J

J - Jesenice to Zagreb – on the EN Zürichsee

Route: Jesenice – Lesce-Bled – Kranj – Ljubljana – Zidani Most – Sevnica – Dobova - Zagreb

Jesenice is probably not a place many readers outside of the Balkans will have heard of. I never had either but I wanted to visit Lake Bled and had heard hotels in Bled itself were astronomically expensive and that it was much better to stay a short train ride away in Jesenice, the first town in Slovenia when crossing from Villach in Austria. Although this is broadly true, it is in fact possible to find decently priced accommodation there but I didn't find this out till another visit some years later.

Jesenice itself is a small industrial town famed for being the home of Slovenian mining and iron production (just saying). When I was there in the 1990s, this was all very believable. Coming from the Midlands (don't know if I've mentioned that), it could very easily have been a small town in the Black Country of yesteryear in terms of grot factor and general down-in-the-mouthness. With one big exception – phenomenal views of the Karavank Alps which form the Austrian-Slovenian border for quite a stretch at this point. As Jesenice is a border town, most people just pass through on their way south to other former Yugoslav destinations, and this isn't entirely a bad thing as there are certainly far more attractive and interesting towns in Slovenia. That said, it's not entirely devoid of charm or attractions. The local delicacies weren't necessarily among them - I remember looking for something to eat in a little restaurant cafe and surveying the menu - 'hog's testicles in own grease' was a new one on me, and though I'd give most things a go, I passed on that. If they'd been in someone else's grease, I might have been more inclined. Maybe I missed out on a real treat – we'll never know.

Nearby Bled, however, certainly was a treat. It's only fifteen minutes from Jesenice and although the station (Lesce-Bled) is about 4 km outside the town, there are plenty of buses and taxis to get you there. The picture postcard views of the lake, its little island and the surrounding mountains are of course the main attraction, and stunning does not do it justice at all. I spent a couple of hours walking around it; from every vantage point it only seemed to look more and more beautiful, my jaw dropping further with each changing angle and vista. I'd already used up half a roll of camera film (remember them?) in the first ten minutes. By contrast, the town itself is oddly unremarkable. There's absolutely nothing wrong with it, it's just very ordinary and modern-looking, with its concrete shopping precinct and car park. But given the beauty of what lies nearby, it can be more than forgiven for being on the plain side. After a lovely day of both visual and gastronomic feasting (and avoiding the hog's testicles), it was back to Jesenice for the night before venturing further south to Zagreb early the next morning.

It's only about 200 km from Jesenice to Zagreb, and I wanted to get there at a reasonable hour to have a fairly full day to explore. Fortunately, there was a train that left Jesenice at around 7.00 a.m., arriving after 10.00 and that seemed like an excellent option. The train was the overnight Belgrade-bound service from Zürich – the EuroNight 'Zürichsee' – which also had seating accommodation for day travellers (or those prepared for a fairly uncomfortable night). In those days, it was still possible to board the majority of international trains without having a reservation (with the exception of couchettes and sleepers, of course), something which on the whole is becoming much harder these days in many countries, particularly on high-speed and/or EuroCity/EuroNight trains.

EuroCity (EC) is the name for a category of cross-border European trains that meet certain internationally agreed criteria regarding speed, quality, comfort, etc. In practice this means they are generally fast, make relatively short stops in major cities only, and you can get something to eat and drink from the dining car. It also means that in most countries, passengers have to pay a sometimes hefty supplement for this hike in quality. They were first introduced back in 1987 as a replacement for the former Trans Europe Express (TEE) services. By that point, the TEE network had practically shrivelled to a handful of services. Part of the problem was that TEE trains offered first class travel only and, while this air of exclusivity had served them well in earlier decades, their popularity began to dwindle among a more cost-conscious mass public who increasingly had faster and cheaper alternatives. EC trains were billed as the modern successor, offering an expanded network of services with air-conditioned first *and* second class accommodation. When they were first introduced, there were also a number of EC night trains, such as the EC Alfred Nobel from Hamburg to Stockholm and Oslo. In 1993, it was agreed that EC trains should complete their journeys between 6.00 a.m. and midnight, so from that year, EC night trains have carried the EuroNight (EN) designation.

Waiting on the platform in Jesenice that morning, I was beginning to regret opting for such an early start. It all looked fairly bleak and desolate at the station with hardly anyone else around. But the train's imminent arrival was soon announced and in it came, accompanied by a flurry of activity as customs and border guards got on and off, and railway workers cracked on with an engine change. I soon found a carriage that was nice and quiet, and my morning journey down to Zagreb lived up to the EuroCity guarantee of being a very comfortable and enjoyable ride. This particular stretch also happens to be a very scenic run – in fact for many years, the *Thomas Cook European Timetable* listed the section between Ljubljana and Zagreb among the most scenic routes in

Europe. Much of the route follows the River Sava, and there are enchanting views of the river, green hills and rugged gorges for much of the way. The Slovenian fields and meadows were charmingly dotted with the little roofed hayracks or 'kozolec' that have become a symbol of the country's national identity.

Arriving on time mid-morning was great and gave me plenty of time to explore Zagreb – just as well, as it was experiencing a full-on Balkan heat-wave at the time, and there was no way I was rushing round in those temperatures. I'm not sure I'd be desperate to rush back to Zagreb, but I did like the city. Maybe it was because of the incredibly hot weather (which meant that anyone with any sense was keeping cool indoors or elsewhere) but it seemed a rather subdued capital. That was all to the good in my book – struggling around in the heat among massive crowds is rarely a joy, so it was nice to be able to stroll around the city centre and take in the sights without having to dodge the masses. The city had a very Austro-Hungarian feel, and the reason for this is of course the obvious one (i.e. it was once part of the Austro-Hungarian Empire). Sipping beers and people watching on the beautiful Ban Jelacic Square was delightful and the rest of the day slipped by just 'heatwave chilling' and sauntering. It's a shame that my single most abiding memory of my time in Zagreb was of the night that followed – sweltering in a hotbox of a room in a high-rise hotel that felt more like a Japanese TV endurance challenge. I can honestly say it was one of the hottest nights I've ever had in my life... and not in a good way.

Train travel thoughts J

Don't be an unadventurous old fart like me – try the hog's testicles and expand your horizons (ancient Chinese proverb).

Early morning trains might seem a pain initially but you can catch up on sleep en route and arrive with plenty of time to sightsee.

K

K1 - Krakow to Berlin - on D 448

Route: Krakow – Katowice – Wroclaw – Rzepin – Frankfurt/Oder - Berlin

I'd had a thoroughly enjoyable few days in Krakow and really took to the city. Marek, my Polish friend from Warsaw, had come down and invited me to stay with him and his wife, Beata. His father was a civil servant and had arranged somewhere for us to stay – via a colleague, who'd spoken to a friend, who'd had a word with an acquaintance, type of thing. It turned out the accommodation was in an annex to one of Krakow's prisons - not one of the trendy converted ones you can now stay in in places like Helsinki or Oxford, but an actual 'working' prison. This is not the sort of place you'd ordinarily think of giving a go if it came up on Booking.com or such like (though I dare say it might be more popular than I expect). Getting in and out was a tad unsettling, and not least because collecting the keys on first arrival involved a short trip through a cell-lined corridor that put me in mind of Clarice's first visit to Hannibal Lektor in *Silence of the Lambs*. Not normally the way you expect a short break to start. Anyway, once we were in, it was a pretty decent set of rooms, even if the setting was admittedly a touch unconventional. This was summer, so the city was baking, and the city-centre cafes were full of tourists enjoying a drink and some relaxation.

This again was during the 1990s and my first visit there.

At this point in time, it still hadn't fully hit the tourist radar and wasn't struggling with the massive overtourism that has plagued it for the last twenty years or so, particularly in the summer months. I'm not surprised so many people want to go there; it's just delightful with its medieval town centre, the old market square, Wawel Cathedral and Castle, and the famously enchanting Cloth Hall, to name but a handful of its many sights. It's a perfect place to saunter around, stopping off to enjoy a drink or bite to eat and admire its easy charms. After a few delightful days, however, it was time to head off once again, this time on to Berlin.

Today, there are a number of fast, direct services between the two cities, meaning that travelling by night is no longer an option or necessity. But at that point in the 1990s, the night train still ran, taking a full ten hours from 21.00 till 7.00 the next morning. The service I was booked on was the unimaginatively unnamed D 448 service which eventually ceased running in 2004. I don't know why, but I tend to fall into the trap of thinking that there won't be many people doing the journey at the same time as me. Why I do this, I don't know, because nine times out of ten I'm wrong and this was one of those occasions. Clearly, the world and his or her wife/husband had decided to join me that night and the train was packed to the rafters. Once again, I'd booked into a six-berth compartment and was accompanied by five fellow travellers. Every one of them appeared to be trying to transport their life-long possessions to Germany, so the compartment had the appearance of a guard's van full of luggage and assorted boxes, over which we were all constantly climbing and jumping every time one of us came in or out. The corridors were full, the vestibules at the end of the carriages were full, the dining car was full, the toilets were constantly engaged. And it was hot. Yet again, I wondered why I was doing this when I could have travelled by day, seen a bit of the countryside and had a more relaxing journey (in theory). These were my thoughts again when I finally managed to take advantage of the end-of-carriage toilet's brief vacant period – only to find the floor swimming (best not to wonder with what), no actual running water where it should have been, no toilet paper, the loo blocked, and a general vibe akin to what I imagine the inmates' toilets might have been like back in Krakow prison.

By the time I got back to the compartment, some of my couchette companions had decided to use my bunk for storage purposes. They must have seen my expression earlier and decided I'd thought better of things. So there I was, back, with an even less inclined expression, no doubt. Though it should have been obvious I would actually need to get back onto my bunk, this seemed to be an unpredictable revelation to my fellow travellers, who only moved their stuff once asked to – and then with huge reluctance and sighs of severe indignation (excuse *me*!). This whole experience could not have been further removed from romantic notions of glamorous night train travel. On top of all this, there was of course the odour challenge to contend with – BO pervaded the compartment (pretty sure it wasn't me), and every time the door was opened, the train loos did their best to add wafts of 'eau de toilette' of the worst kind. And again, ten hours of this.... Two of the passengers amazed me by engaging in constant conversation for the duration of the journey. As I lay there, coming in and out of light sleep, I wondered how people could actually sustain a conversation for that amount of time. What is there to talk about? Surely at some point they'll throw the conversational towel in and want to get some sleep, I thought – but no. I could go on, but reliving this experience is starting to unsettle me and I'm sure you've got the impression by now – it wasn't the most restful night ever.

Despite this particular journey ending up as a bit of a trial, train services between Poland and Germany have always been decent in terms of number and frequency, even in Communist times – when ironically there were even more direct connections (e.g. between Munich and Warsaw, Cologne and Krakow, etc). Today, the Berlin Warsaw Express runs four times a day in each direction, and several other trains provide direct connections between Berlin and cities such as Stettin, Katowice and Krakow. But, as with all journeys, the end was approaching and thoughts of the trying night were also coming to an end as we moved through Berlin's eastern suburbs. Yet again, I have to confess to a feeling of real excitement, reaching Berlin for the first time, and thinking of Brian Roberts – the character played by Michael York in the 1972 film *Cabaret* (one of my all-time favourite films).

Just like him, I was full of anticipation as we finally pulled into Germany's capital city (Brian had of course arrived on the train from the Hook of Holland). Though the city's dark side only grew grimmer back then, the decadent air and flair of 1930s Berlin is still a powerful and more positive image, helped of course by the ongoing traction of productions like *Cabaret* and continued interest in the various writings of Christopher Isherwood. Naively, I was hoping to sense something of all this as I walked around the city. In reality of course, modern Berlin is inevitably a very different place, however much certain clubs and venues attempt to recreate an air of that 1930s Bohemianism. That said, I think it would be hard not to be impressed by Berlin. It wears its history unselfconsciously on its sleeve; echoes of the Second World War are everywhere but the city has worked its way through years of therapy and ended up as a dynamic forward-looking metropolis. As gratifying as it was to see the Wall down and its status as fully-fledged capital restored, I couldn't help but feel sorry this was my first visit; why had I left it so late to go there? It must have been quite something to have been there during Cold

War times and experience it as the divided city it had once been. As a teacher of German at the time, I felt even more remiss for never having been before, but what can you do? And despite my best intentions, I've not been back since. Time to do something about that, I think, but it certainly won't be a trip on the D 448....

K2 - Kehl to Strasbourg – on the local shuttle

Route: Kehl – Strasbourg!

At ten minutes, this is the shortest trip in the book. Strasbourg will no doubt be a familiar name to most people but I'd be surprised if Kehl rings a bell. In fact most people I mentioned this trip to thought I meant Kiel in north Germany (the German pronunciation of the two names is awkwardly close). But Kehl is the small German border town on the opposite side of the Rhine to Strasbourg, the mighty Rhine Bridge lying between them. In one way it's a little surprising it's such a relatively unknown place (outside of Germany) because for well over a hundred years, Strasbourg-Kehl has been the principal border crossing for trains passing between France and Germany. This is partly because long-distance trains coming from northern and eastern Germany (i.e. Berlin, Hamburg, Dortmund and Cologne, etc) have tended to enter France via Belgium, while a relatively smaller number of trains from central Germany and further afield (Prague and Frankfurt) tended to cross the border slightly further north at Forbach/Saarbrücken.

But its status as principal crossing point is certainly reflected in the number of international trains that once called there, as the following table shows:

Train name	From/to	From/to
-	Strasbourg	Salzburg/Hof/Lindau
-	Frankfurt/Dortmund	Port Bou/Marseille/Ventimiglia
-	Frankfurt/Dortmund	St Gervais/Bourg St Maurice
Albert Schweitzer TEE/EC	Lyon/Strasbourg	Dortmund/Stuttgart
EC services (unnamed)	Paris	Stuttgart/Munich
InterRegio (IR) services	Strasbourg	All German destinations
Maurice Ravel (EC)	Paris	Munich
Mozart (FD/D/EC)	Paris	Vienna
Orient Express	Paris	Vienna/Budapest/Bucharest

Given changes in Schengen arrangements, long distance trains from France no longer stopped in Kehl after 2013, and the much truncated remnant of the Orient Express pulled in for the last time on 14th December 2009. Nonetheless, local shuttles still operate back and forth between the two places, and a relatively new tram service also connects them these days.

So, a small but interesting snippet of international railway history. But why am I mentioning this, you may well ask. The answer has to do with my family and, in particular, my niece and nephew, Kate and Matthew. Around twenty or so years ago they were at school and studying French (Matthew) and German (Kate) for their GCSEs. As they'd never been to France or Germany, Margaret thought it'd be a nice idea for us all (my sister Diane included) to spend part of the summer holidays somewhere along the French-German border where we could nip backwards and forwards and give the kids a chance to have a stab at communicating with the locals. Kehl came to mind as a place that fitted the bill; I looked into accommodation options and found an apartment right in the centre of the old town – and what an absolutely beautiful little old town it is, with its cluster of black, red and white half-timbered houses. Classic chocolate box beauty maybe, but still lovely to look at and to spend time in.

The weather was very good, the locals were friendly (and happy to let Kate practise her German with them), the food was fab – what more can you ask for? Ok, the old church opposite chimed very loudly every fifteen minutes and the mosquitoes were living life and loving it, but there always has to be something, and they were very minor somethings in my book. It was a pleasant walk past fields of ripening maize to get to Kehl station and, with several trains an hour over the border, it couldn't have been easier. Standing waiting on the platform was quite a thrill (for me again, at least) with goods trains thundering through at high-speed. I imagined the Orient Express pulling up here on its way from Paris to Munich, Vienna, Budapest and Bucharest. Back in the day, border guards and customs officials must have had quite a presence at the station. But at this point in the early 2000s, it was a very quiet country stop that belied the status it once held as Germany's chief western gatekeeper.

We hopped onto the local shuttle when it came in and were soon crossing the Rhine and on our way to France. The new bridge that was finished in 2010 can now accommodate high-speed trains crossing at a speed of 120 km/h; the maximum speed prior to this was just 60 km/h. As a result, the city of Karlsruhe is generally now the first stop in Germany after leaving Strasbourg. But the local shuttle bobbed us along gently so we had time to take in the views of the Rhine. I don't think anyone would describe it as overly scenic at this point; in fact, it's strangely unremarkable. And that somehow made it all the more difficult to grasp how a border that has been such a frequent point of historical conflict and dispute could now look so ordinary. But that's the things with borders – invisible political constructs often fraught with complex histories and chequered pasts; yet in most cases in the EU today, less marked than ever. It's possible to walk across the new bridge (the Europe Bridge) and stand with a foot in each country – I'm sure there must be thousands of photos of people doing exactly that.

I was still reflecting on all this as we pulled into Strasbourg's immense station and navigated our way out into the city. I really like Strasbourg, with its Gothic cathedral, medieval bridges, Kleber Square and the beautiful Petite France district. The local Alsatian cuisine is wonderful, if not a bit formidable in the sausage and meat department, and definitely more appealing in winter than on a hot summer's day. It's sad that the city's name, a bit like Brussels, has ended up as a negative shorthand for anti-EU sentiment in parts of the UK press and media because it really is a delightful city, whatever your politics. Just be careful what you order to eat though, especially if you're not sure whether you're in or out on fermented cabbage, poached liver dumplings and pork knuckles.

Train travel thoughts K

Ear plugs/phones can be an absolute blessing in shared couchettes.

Did I mention the vapour rub trick before?

Always travel with tissues and a spare loo roll. Preferably discreetly packed.

We can travel practically anywhere, except into the past...if you want to see the present, don't leave it till the future.

Mosquito repellent is always a handy thing to remember.

L

L1 - Lichfield to Antwerp – on just about anything going

Route: Lichfield – Birmingham – London Euston/Victoria – Dover – Calais – Ostend – Bruges – Ghent - Antwerp

This journey was supposed to be a gentle start to an Interrail trip, and the plan for day one was to get as far as Amsterdam to stay with my friend Paul for a couple of nights before heading on up to Denmark. In a nutshell, it didn't happen – at least not on day one, but more of that shortly.

If I've understood things correctly, Eurostar can now be included as part of your outbound/ inbound Interrail trip. I'm not entirely sure if that's always been the case and, if it has, I didn't know about it. As a veteran of ferry travel, my automatic MO was to get down to Dover, cross the Channel, and on we go. At the time of this particular trip, I was living just outside Lichfield to the north of Birmingham. As was the case for lots of people who live in towns just north of the city, travelling south usually meant getting a fairly slow local connection to Birmingham New Street, where you could then pick up a fast service to London Euston. One key advantage of Lichfield is that there are very occasional direct West Coast services coming from further north that stop at

Trent Valley station and then go on, sometimes even without stopping, straight to London. One of these services was an early morning train at around 8.00 and the beauty of this was that it meant I could arrive in London in good time to make the relevant onward connections and get to Amsterdam at a reasonable hour. That was at least the theory. As we know though, things so often just go wrong.

There's always something very unsettling about delay announcements that keep coming, each time adding on another five minutes. The platform at Lichfield became fuller by the minute, the delay notifications continued; 8.00 became 9.00. An hour seems a very long time of course when you're expecting an imminent arrival. Some time after 9.00, it was announced that the direct service had in fact been cancelled and passengers would need to get the next local service to New Street. In an instant, I knew this meant the whole day's travel plans were most likely up the swanny. The word was that refunds, food vouchers and compensation could be claimed from the Virgin office in Birmingham. Mass groaning and moaning spread like wildfire on the platform, and only got worse when seemingly hundreds of passengers tried to cram themselves onto the next local train to New Street. Inevitably, it was standing room only for most of us, faces virtually pressed up against the glass, and grappling for a hand-hold at every jolt – we've all been there. Thank God it was only a forty minute journey.

It was well after 10.00 when the train finally pulled into Birmingham. Had things gone according to plan, I'd have been well on my way to London Victoria by this point. Because I had a good half an hour before the next train to Euston, I thought I'd look in on the Virgin office to see what was what. In an instant, I knew it wasn't worth bothering - an immense queue snaked out of the office where a couple of pubescent reps slowly dealt with the angry hordes. Sometimes life really is just too short. I always find it difficult to be sanguine in moments like this – it's not the end of the world, there are people dealing with far worse.... and yet I find myself consumed with rage and disgruntlement. (Note to self – relax.) Before too much longer, I was on the next Virgin train to Euston, which was itself delayed on arrival at New Street, and got further delayed for reasons unknown en route; the apologies announced were hugely appreciated by all.

After what seemed like several months, I was navigating my way through the pitch invasion experience that Euston prides itself on, muttering like a semi-finalist on *Britain's Got Grumpy Bastards*. So began the delightful next leg, the underground trek to Victoria Station. Once there, I realised there was a train to Dover leaving quite soon. It's always a calculated gamble in this situation – is it worth bothering risking a heart attack on the outside chance of managing to catch it, or do you resign yourself to the delay and get the next one at your leisure? Despite my better judgement, I opted for the first plan – and predictably, saw the train leaving the platform just as I got to it, sweating and panting like a vicar with a questionable hard-drive. Hey-ho. This day was not shaping up as I'd planned, and this of course meant yet another delay, waiting for the next service.

Eventually I was en route for Dover and, after a couple of hours, boarding the ferry bound for Ostend – yippee! At least I could relax for a few hours and have a look round on deck. It seemed in no hurry to depart, so I was relieved to feel it finally moving off. Some time into the crossing, yet another announcement – due to 'issues' at the port in Ostend, the ferry was being diverted to Calais where coaches would be waiting for onward transport by road to Belgium. Not yippee. Getting to Amsterdam by nightfall was looking ever more unlikely. In Calais, I joined the queue for passport control. Seeing the border guard glancing doubtfully from my face to my photograph, I couldn't help but say, "Yes, that's what I looked like when I left home this morning". I think they're specially trained to ignore amusing quips.

Days like this really make you wonder why you've bothered, but you have to be firm with yourself and remember the fun that travelling by train can be. And now that Eurostar has vastly simplified the London to Paris route, such experiences are by and large a thing of the past (see L2 below). In fact, lots of the cross-channel ferry routes no longer even accommodate foot passengers, the vast majority of whom were rail passengers in the 1990s and before. Once through customs, more waiting followed, and the coaches finally turned up for the 100 km drive along to Ostend. By this point, ridiculously, it was around 8.30 pm. I quickly checked train times and realised it wouldn't be possible to get to Amsterdam that night. So I rang Paul from a phone box at the station (once I managed to get some Belgian coins - thank the Lord for mobile phones nowadays) and Antwerp looked like the best bet for the night. Not where I wanted to be, though it is a lovely city, but just disappointing when had things gone to plan, I'd have been enjoying a beer in Amsterdam several hours ago.

I got to Antwerp in just under two hours and decided to look for a cheap hotel near the station. Not the best time of night to be looking and the first few I tried had no vacancies... once more, thoughts of never doing this again filled my mind. After much trudging (*mudging*? You heard it here first), I got a room in a place that I would never have chosen on Booking.com, but what can you do? It had a bed, I was exhausted and fed up, and in the mood for chips and a good night's sleep. The good night was marred by the loud music coming up from the bar below and just continued the vibe of the day. I lay on my bed and tried to be zen about it all – sometimes that is all you can do. Tomorrow would be a better day and Amsterdam would be a relatively short ninety minute train ride away – I'd had some Belgian frites and a strong beer – smile and put the day behind you!

L2 - London to Paris and Brussels – on Eurostar

Route: London Waterloo/St Pancras – Lille Europe – Brussels/Paris

I felt I had to include a section on Eurostar, if only because it's been such a landmark railway achievement. When I was growing up, the idea of building a Channel Tunnel would occasionally be aired on television and the conclusion of every documentary always seemed to be that it was ultimately the stuff of fantasy. For most of my youth, it seemed to be one of those ideas in the same bag as the fall of the Iron Curtain and the reunification of Germany – unlikely ever to happen in our lifetime. And then suddenly... As we all know, it's now a reality and celebrating its 30th anniversary in 2024.

My first time on Eurostar was a short break to Paris back in 1995, just a year after it had been launched. I've travelled on it a fair few times to Brussels since then, and even after all this time I can't seem to get over the shock factor – how can we get there so quickly? I know that's a ridiculous question – it's a high-speed train using special tracks and going through an undersea tunnel. But after so many old-style Channel crossings where it seemed to take forever, I genuinely still have trouble processing what a straightforwardly fast service it is.

As anyone who's done the old train and ferry routes

knows, London to Paris was generally a seven to eight hour undertaking during the day – or the whole of an awful night for the very brave/foolish. And it wasn't just the time – it was the whole palaver of bus transfers at Dover, on top of the lengthy train journeys either side of the Channel (see L1 – Lichfield to Antwerp above). Even using the fast service by hovercraft didn't really make a huge difference. Admittedly, it reduced the Channel crossing to thirty-five minutes but this gain was offset by bus transfers between trains and the hoverports.

It was a similar story with London to Brussels – a journey of over seven to eight hours by day and nine by night. The ferry to Ostend was, of course, a longer trip at about four hours but a shorter train run from Ostend. The introduction of the jetfoil was quite a significant timesaving on this route, reducing it to just over five hours, but it often got cancelled if the sea looked a bit choppy, and then it was back on the ferry. So the fact that you can get to both cities in just over two hours today is still something I struggle to take in. I've never done the London to Amsterdam route, which takes around four hours, but this too fills me with awe, as I'm sure it does anyone who ever did the Liverpool Street – Harwich – Hook – Amsterdam run (a nine hour game by day or twelve by night).

Just thinking back to my first London to Brussels trip on Eurostar: I'd contacted Belgian Rail to enquire about the possibility of obtaining some of the destination signs I collect. They passed me on to the man in charge of the depot at Bruxelles Midi station who kindly invited me to visit – result! I headed down to London to stay overnight at a friend's and got the first train out the next morning. I snoozed through the Kent countryside and woke up just before Brussels. Soon enough, I was on my way to the depot and, once there, loading the old signs they'd kept for me into the empty suitcase I had taken for this purpose. I was of course in collectors' heaven (things like this happen very rarely), and it was one of those lovely times in life where the kindness of strangers seems so life-affirming. The 'depot guys' and I chatted away, enjoying a coffee and a bit of bonhomie; they shared all sorts of yesteryear tales of working on the railways – bumping into Audrey Hepburn getting off the overnight express from Venice; an American tourist mysteriously found dead in a sleeping car on the Ost West Express; and the time an Ostend-Cologne carriage, complete with passengers, mistakenly ended up in Luxembourg. After a while, I was conscious of taking up too much of their time, so went off for a walk to reacquaint myself with the city. I went to the beautiful Grande Place for some lunch and a Belgian beer by the fire in one of the old Guild House cafes that line the square. And then back to Midi station to collect my case, a quick 'au revoir' to my new depot chums, and back to London on the afternoon Eurostar. I was back in the Midlands that evening, still struggling to believe it'd been possible to get to Brussels and back in a day.

I should mention that from the late 1930s to 1980 (notwithstanding certain periods of suspension), it had of course been possible to travel direct from London Victoria to Paris and Brussels on the old *Night Ferry*. This must have been a really civilised way to travel overnight, though still quite a long haul at around eleven hours. The trains consisted exclusively of sleepers which were clamped down onto the ferry at Dover for onward travel to Dunkirk, and then on to the two capitals via Lille. In some periods there were even direct carriages from London to Basle in Switzerland – an amazing thought.

Eurostar may be fast but it does of course have its problems. The whole checking in and out procedure can be a trial at times and limited waiting capacity in the departure and arrival areas often makes delays and cancellations a bit of a travel nightmare, to say the least. But when it works, it's fabulous – fast, comfortable and enjoyable. It's also meant that onward journeys to many other European destinations (thanks partly to high-speed improvements elsewhere) can now easily be completed before nightfall, even to cities as far away as Milan or Barcelona.

One big disappointment for many folks like me living north of London was the abandoning of plans for the originally proposed Regional Eurostar services. This would have meant direct trains from cities like Birmingham, Manchester and Glasgow to Paris and Brussels. The rolling stock (98 carriages) for these trains was in fact commissioned and built but the services were never introduced – partly because the timing and economics weren't great (coinciding with the explosion in cheap air fares) and partly because of the lack of political will; I wonder if this might have been viewed differently now in light of the more recent focus on 'levelling up' ... but probably not. There had even been plans for international sleeper trains on some of the regional routes (Nightstar) but, as we know, they also never came about. All sorts of concerns were raised, e.g., about the additional weight of water services on trains via the Chunnel. You'd think these considerations might have been aired and shared before the trains were built, abandoned and then sold off to Canada. But we live and learn (apparently).

As something of a sop to disappointed northerners, two 'Eurostar Link' trains were introduced in 1995/96. These ran once a day from Edinburgh (via the East Coast route) and Manchester (via the West Coast line) to connect directly with London Waterloo, saving passengers from the north the hassle of getting from Euston and King's Cross. Unless the departure time of your Eurostar conveniently matched the Link's arrival, however, they weren't much use at one train a day... and so they too were soon abandoned. Switching the Eurostar terminal to St Pancras has admittedly been a welcome development for some, but for many like myself arriving at Euston or other London termini, the kerfuffle factor remains intact.

But despite these disappointments, Eurostar is still a phenomenal improvement and who knows what additional services and routes might come along in the future.

Train travel thoughts L

It's rare for everything to be plain sailing on an Interrail trip; as and when something does go wrong, try to go with the flow – things always get sorted out in the end.

If you can't be zen, get a bag of chips (get chips anyway).

M

M1 - Moscow to London – on the Ost West Express (East West Express)

Route: Moscow – Viazma – Smolensk – Orsha – Minsk – Brest – Terespol – Warsaw – Poznan – Kunowice – Frankfurt/Oder – Berlin Schönefeld Airport – Marienborn – Helmstedt – Hanover – Dortmund – Dusseldorf – Cologne – Aachen - Liège – Brussels – Ghent – Bruges – Ostend – London

At a distance of around 2700 km to Ostend, this is the longest continuous train journey I've ever been on. At the time (thirty plus years ago now), Moscow was still one of the best connected places on the planet in terms of the number of direct international destinations available from the city. This was largely down to a system of carefully crafted timetable manoeuvres that meant direct through coaches were sent on journeys all over Europe and Asia, piggy-backing on various other services as they travelled. In many cases there was often just a solitary Soviet/Russian Railways (S/RZD) sleeper carriage that covered the entire journey. The direct sleeper connection between Moscow and Oslo is a good example; the carriage travelled west on a Moscow-Berlin service. Once it arrived in Berlin it was uncoupled and connected to a Berlin-Malmö service. On arrival in Sweden, it was uncoupled again and this time re-attached to a Malmö-Gothenburg-Oslo service. Similar manoeuvres happened all over the Continent and, for many years, such moves were a common part of railway practice (and headaches too, no doubt, especially when connecting services were delayed or disrupted). Since then, long distance operations such as these have sadly been hugely reduced, but up until the early 1990s it meant you could travel from – for example - central Spain to North Korea with just one change of train in Moscow – a journey of roughly 10,000 km. This is all the more amazing when you think that a train journey from Wolverhampton to Norwich back then often meant changing at least three or four times.

Just to illustrate the diversity and number of connections from Moscow, the table below shows a selection of the direct rail destinations available from the city in 1993, and the time taken.

Direct through coach from Moscow to:	Time taken (approximately)
Athens	66 hours
Beijing	5-6 days (depending on route)
Belgrade	43 hours
Berlin	28 hours
Bern	46 hours

Bratislava	38 hours
Bucharest	35 hours
Budapest	34 hours
Copenhagen	40 hours
Frankfurt	40 hours
Geneva	49 hours
Helsinki	15 hours
Hook of Holland	40 hours
Istanbul	62 hours
Jolfa (Iran)	65 hours
Madrid	89 hours
Malmö	40 hours
Ostend	42 hours
Oslo	51 hours
Paris	43 hours
Prague	42 hours
Pyongyang	6-7 days (depending on route)
Rome	62 hours

Sofia	45 hours
Ulaanbaatar	4 days
Vienna	34 hours
Warsaw	18 hours
Zagreb	43 hours

Our journey back from Russia on the East West Express was also a good illustration of this practice. We were in the single sleeping car heading for Brussels and Ostend. As for the other carriages, some went only as far as Minsk, while others completed their journey in Warsaw or Berlin. At Aachen, most of the remaining carriages headed on to the Gare du Nord in Paris. Our carriage was uncoupled and attached to a Cologne – Ostend service. As previously mentioned, most of these long distance connections dwindled to virtually nothing during the 90s, though RZD did have something of a short-lived international comeback in 2010. New sleeper trains with impressive new rolling stock were launched from Moscow to such destinations as Amsterdam, Brussels and Vienna. This initiative was driven almost more by Russian political posturing – sending out visible symbols of Russian influence into the West – than by actual customer demand, however. As such, most of the services were suspended after a couple of years, though the *Trans-European Express* (Moscow – Minsk – Warsaw – Berlin – Frankfurt – Strasbourg – Paris) and the service to Nice via Vienna fared much better, surviving until the 2020 Covid pandemic.

Going back to 1993, Margaret and I had spent an interesting few weeks travelling by train in Russia. At this time in the early 1990s, the country was very much in the early stages of reinventing itself and moving away from its Communist past. This process was not easy, and there were burgeoning signs everywhere of a new entrepreneurialism that sat very uncomfortably alongside the more dominant impression of mass poverty. It was shocking to see elderly women standing on street corners trying to sell an old banana or household possessions in order to get by. After a time, the constant confrontation with poverty and desperation made the whole experience of being in Russia rather dispiriting. Staying with a number of families, we saw this up close and had to admire their resolve, ingenuity and spirit. It's such a shame that ordinary Russians are still suffering thirty years on, perhaps even more tethered and limited because of the current regime's policies and priorities.

Before our visit, a Russian friend had advised us to dress down on our travels (not that we had any designer togs anyway). Her advice was based on the need to blend in with ordinary locals, as standing out as Westerners at the time could have made us easy targets for opportunist thieves. We clearly managed to follow her advice very well; on one occasion, we stood window-shopping outside what was clearly a swanky new bookshop. Suddenly, a security guard came out muttering something in Russian that sounded none too friendly – a friend translated – 'Clear off, you're lowering the tone and you couldn't afford anything here anyway!' Charmed, I'm sure.

So one way or another, being in Moscow had felt quite overwhelming. The amazing architecture and generous hospitality couldn't really compensate for the oppressive scale of this massive city, the poverty, pollution and the drab austerity that choked the place. So when it was time to head home on the East West Express, we were not sorry, as interesting an experience as it had been in many ways. As the train pulled out of Moscow's huge Belorusskaya Station at around 18.30 that Saturday evening, I have to confess to breathing a small sigh of relief. We'd booked a sleeper for the two of us, and though it was far from luxurious, it felt wonderful having our own space and knowing we were on our way back home, even though we'd be on the train for nearly two days. Tea was available from the huge samovar in the attendant's or 'provodnik's' compartment at the end of the carriage but there was no catering, so we'd packed a few provisions to tide us over.

Before too long, we were out of the endless Moscow suburbs and into the Russian countryside – views of flat fields and trees that didn't much change the entire length of the journey across the North European Plain, making this not a particularly scenic journey. As evening turned to night, we crossed into Belarus, a country that had only declared its independence from the USSR a couple of years before. I remember arriving in Minsk at around 5.00 the next morning, and the strange metallic blast from the tannoy announcing Minsk Pasażyrski Station. Eventually I drifted back off, and at around 9.30, we reached the Belarusian border town of Brest. This was a very lengthy stop of about three hours. The reason for this was the gauge difference between that used in the former USSR and the rest of Europe; because of the difference, each train carriage had to be uncoupled, mechanically hoisted up, and then fitted with a new set of bogies for onward travel into Poland and Western Europe – a time-consuming process that still happens to this day. At around 12.30, we were back on track (literally) and heading into Poland, putting our watches back an hour. At around 14.45, we pulled into Warsaw's East Station (Warszawa Wschodnia) for another fairly lengthy stop. Our Polish friends, Marek and Beata, got on here, eager to catch up with us on our time in Russia. They'd also very kindly brought us a selection of bread rolls, drinks and snacks for the rest of the journey.

After that, afternoon gradually turned into evening, the passing scenery unchanging. One amazing thing I found about doing a lengthy train journey like this is that you really relax. I've been on ninety minute flights where I watch the passing of every minute, sitting there impatiently and fretting about every short delay. But on a train for two days, this way of thinking goes out of the window, and I manage to become more zen than ever. I've heard people say they experienced this even more intensely on longer train trips, such as on the *Trans-Siberian Express*. I suppose the knowledge that this isn't a short trip lulls you into a more accepting and peaceful frame of mind somehow. I was reflecting on this when we finally reached Germany's eastern border at Frankfurt an der Oder at just after 23.00 that Sunday evening – when my sense of inner calm was about to be tested.

As usual, customs and border guards came through the train, inspecting tickets and passports. Suddenly, we heard what sounded like very tense exchanges a few compartments further along. We'd had a few chats with several fellow passengers so were aware that some of the Russians on the train were badminton players heading to an international tournament in Liège. It turned out they didn't have a transit visa for Germany. Despite their pleas and evidence of their upcoming participation in the games, the German guards were having none of it. The discussions turned into full-blown arguments which culminated in very angry shouting and eventually, in the border guards turfing the Russian players off the train, shouting 'Raus, raus!' and telling the hapless Russians to go back to the German Embassy in Moscow to organise their visas. Our hearts went out to them – admittedly, they'd slipped up, but how awful that after about thirty hours on the train, they were unceremoniously manhandled off onto the station platform close to midnight, having to wait God knows how long for the long journey back home... and missing out on a tournament that they'd no doubt been preparing for for many months. The whole incident was grim and left us unsettled and untalkative. The sight of armed, uniformed Germans screaming at foreign travellers inevitably conjured up unsavoury thoughts and associations.

This hadn't been the perfect recipe for a good night's sleep, and I remember lying there still awake when the train made a short stop at Berlin Schönefeld Airport at around half past midnight. Eventually I drifted off, and thought about the poor Russians again when we arrived in Liège around 10.00 on the Monday morning. Brussels soon followed and, at around midday, after two nights on the train, we were finally arriving in Ostend, soon to be boarding the ferry back to Dover followed by the train to London Victoria and an overnight stay with friends. We took a taxi from Victoria to their house, and I'll never forget how startlingly vibrant and colourful London suddenly seemed; it was like seeing it with completely new eyes for the first time, a totally alien world, and a huge contrast with the overall bleakness we'd almost adjusted to. I remember the taxi driver asking where we'd been as we reflected on this; we told him we'd just come back on the train from Russia, feeling incredibly intrepid. 'Have you?' he replied. 'Weather forecast not looking too good here for the next few days....' It's a strange realisation that sometimes people just aren't interested in your stories; it's absolutely fair enough of course, why should they be? We're all wrapped up in the detail of our own days and lives, but ever since then it's made me much more mindful of the small ways in which we can sometimes diminish others by closing down conversations.

M2 - Munich to Salzburg via Berchtesgaden – on the IC Alpenland and regional trains

Route: Munich – Rosenheim – Traunstein – Freilassing – Bad Reichenhall – Bayerisch Gmain - Berchtesgaden – Freilassing – Salzburg

In the days when you could buy Interrail passes by zone, I once bought a two-week pass for Germany, Switzerland and Austria. This was a lovely opportunity to visit lots of places I'd never been to before and, as a German teacher at the time, a chance to see some of the towns I'd been talking about in lessons – the A Level syllabus we were teaching at the time included Bavaria as one of the set topics. The Bavarian Alps really are staggering, it has to be said. I'd also managed to get down to the popular tourist resort of Garmisch-Partenkirchen, not far from the Austrian border, and from where more adventurous souls than me trek up to Germany's highest mountain, the Zugspitze. Taking in the splendid scenery and mountain air was one thing, but my other aim was a Dracula-related mission (sort of). If you've ever seen the 1979 Werner Herzog remake of the classic 1922 vampire film *Nosferatu*, there's an incredible scene where the protagonist, Jonathan Harker, is making his way on foot through what is supposedly the Borgo Pass in the wilds of Transylvania. The scene was actually filmed in the amazing Partnach Gorge just outside Garmisch. As (bad) luck would have it, it turned out to be closed for safety repairs on my visit, owing to some dreadful weather in the preceding days – I'll try again another time. Garmisch itself was still well worth the visit, but after a day or two, it was back to Munich for the next planned leg.

It's very easy to wax lyrical about Munich – such a beautiful, colourful city with so much to see and a vibrant atmosphere. A steady stroll round the old town is a wander through architectural splendour, especially around the Marienplatz with its two beautiful town halls (old and new). I climbed the 300 steps of the Peter's Church from where the views round and about are just amazing, looking over to the onion domes of the Frauenkirche and down to the famous Viktualienmarkt. I used to have a poster of this market on my wall at university, though I'd never been there. Once again, moments like this when travel gives us the chance to close these little loops in life are wonderful and quite moving (or maybe I'm just turning into/have always been a sentimental old fart).

Eventually, it was time to get the afternoon Alpenland

intercity down to Berchtesgaden. I've always loved German IC trains – they always seemed so modern, sleek, fast and efficient, certainly in comparison with UK fast trains of the past, though these are generally much improved today (in many cases). I also loved the fact that every IC train had its own name; quite often these were prominent Germans from history – scientists, artists, writers, and so on - or sometimes the name reflected the geography of its destination, as in this case. An intercity train on this particular route was quite an unusual thing, even then (only local trains operate on the line now). The large number of stops in the various resort towns between Munich and Berchtesgaden meant that the train never really had time to pick up much speed, so it took around three hours to complete the 180 km journey. Not that that remotely bothered me – relaxing in the dining car with a couple of beers, and chatting to the barman while taking in the wonderful Alpine views en route was an absolute treat, and the closer we got to Berchtesgaden, the more spectacular the scenery became.

When I'd mentioned to friends I was planning to visit Berchtesgaden, most people asked me if it was because of an interest in Hitler. A fair enough question, I suppose, given that the Nazi-built 'Eagle's Nest' (or the Kehlsteinhaus in German) famously sits at the top of the Kehlstein, a rocky outcrop high up in the mountains surrounding the town. Amazingly, most of it is still intact and open to tourists, but I have to admit I always feel a bit queasy about visiting places with sinister pasts; I've never been to Auschwitz for the same reason. It's an odd one really, as I love to visit places that are supposedly haunted; but the potential domains of supernatural entities somehow bother me less than sites where documented human atrocities actually took place. In one respect it's a shame I didn't go, as the views are apparently nothing short of spectacular. But even without going up there, the views from all around the town are fabulous – it's no wonder that Berchtesgaden has its own national park named after the town.

It's only about 30 km from there to Salzburg but, because of the terrain, it still takes more than an hour on the train. So the next morning I was off again, this time on a local train back to the border town of Freilassing to get the connection for Salzburg. I wanted to call in briefly at the station there as I knew quite a few international trains stopped here for marshalling purposes. I'm pleased to say the depot workers I spoke to couldn't have been friendlier, and I came away with a nice old destination sign from a sleeper carriage from Salzburg to Ostend (I know, it takes all sorts). I was soon back on the next local shuttle taking me on the short hop across the Austrian border and into Salzburg.

The train approach into Salzburg offers magnificent views of the city; the mighty Hohensalzburg Fortress (one of the biggest castles in Europe) dominates the skyline, and does it in some style. The city certainly makes a grand impression and it's not surprising that the old city centre has been declared a UNESCO World Heritage site. Ok, it is a bit Disney in some ways, and that's nothing to do with its famous *Sound of Music* and Mozart connections. It's just that it's so perfect and pristinely photogenic, especially when you wander round the Mirabell Palace gardens, that it almost feels slightly staged and artificial. Maybe not everyone feels this way, and I don't say this to diminish it in any way, as it really is an impressive and fascinating city. Picking up on the *Sound of Music* connection, I've read that every year around 300,000 people take part in the specially organised city tours showing you where various scenes were filmed and other bits of von Trapp family claptrap. I shouldn't really judge as I appreciate different things float all our boats, but a few beers in the old town seemed far more appealing to me.

M3 - Malaga to Cordoba – on the Seville Avant

Route: Malaga – Antequera-Santa Ana – Puente Genil-Herrera – Cordoba

This was a train trip we went on fairly recently. We'd booked a February break in Malaga for a week's rest and some winter sunshine. Neither David nor I had ever been before and, though we'd booked a decent hotel, I'm ashamed to say I was guilty of having severely misjudged the city. Ever since I was a kid in the 1970s, I'd overheard conversations in supermarkets and bus queues about people flying to Malaga for their holidays in Fuengirola, Marbella and Torremolinos. Rightly or wrongly, these repeated mentions over the years had become associated in my mind with kiss-me-quick fun and all-day breakfast Brit breaks. I only ever seemed to hear mention of sunbeds, lager and sex... (have just booked a fortnight). I knew there must have been far more to the Costa del Sol than this, but hadn't anticipated how absolutely lovely Malaga actually is.

Staying in the old town was a revelation for me and the reality of street after street of occasionally faded but always elegant splendour was a world away from the stereotype I'd built up in my mind. Stately buildings lined beautifully tiled streets and alleyways; old churches hid behind fin-de-siècle façades; the bars, restaurants and coffee houses brought to mind the most sophisticated Parisian equivalents. And this is saying nothing of the impressive historical sights dotted around the centre – the medieval Arabic fortress, the Alacazaba, next to the remains of the Roman amphitheatre; the city's enormous, breathtaking cathedral; and the mighty Gibralfaro castle high up on the hill. For the more culturally inclined, there's also the Picasso museum – I'm doubly ashamed to say I didn't know he was from there and we didn't get round to going. Sometimes, you just can't fit it all in. So in short, take this as my full and signed confession to having grossly under-estimated this marvellous city – lesson well and truly learned.

Despite Malaga offering more than enough for a week's entertainment, I wanted to travel on a Spanish train for the first time and see a bit more of the country. I knew that Cordoba was more than doable for a day-trip, so looked into times and prices. My natural inclination in this sort of situation is just to turn up at the station and buy a ticket. But from experience and research, I realise that these days, that's rarely the best or cheapest way to go about it. So, despite my technophobic tendencies, I went online and booked tickets for an Avant train – a high-speed service used for mid-distances in Spain (Cordoba is about 165 km north of Malaga).

My first surprise on arrival at Malaga Central was the airport style security and scanning arrangements for travellers and their luggage. We'd allowed plenty of time so it wasn't an issue, and I totally understand the need for increased security in this day and age. But I have to acknowledge that with some sadness. That free-and-easy world of rail travel is not quite what it used to be anywhere. From what I gather, in Spain these arrangements tend to apply more to high-speed services than to local trains. But from what we saw in Malaga, every traveller had their luggage scanned and a quick electronic truncheon-type body scan before going through to the platforms.

Once through, we soon found the right platform, where passengers were already forming an orderly queue. Around twenty minutes prior to departure, the barrier opened and a RENFE employee scanned tickets electronically before allowing us through and onto the train. I must admit that this always makes me nervous. Given my penchant for paper, I just don't like e-tickets – I appreciate all the arguments in their favour, but I like something tangible in my hand; I dare say it's partly an age thing. I can never help worrying about whether my phone will open the ticket, whether the scanner will work, and what'll happen if it does all go pear-shaped. Typically, it took three attempts for my ticket to be successfully scanned (everyone else's seemed to work straight off). The five seconds of delay involved equated to a week taken off my life in concentrated worry. Relieved, we moved along and boarded the Seville bound train.

As my first taste of Spanish Railways, it was impressive; the seats were spacious with plenty of legroom, the train was clean, stylish and quiet. We departed right on time and were soon moving through the Andalusian Mountains north of the city. As is probably more than clear by now, I love a great view, and this stretch did not disappoint. Once the hills receded, the scenery gave way to mile after mile of olive groves and the occasional distant castle. High-speed Avant trains like the one we were travelling on are generally used on routes of under 350 km, and have a top speed of around 250 km/h. As such, it was only just over an hour to cover the 100 mile journey. I can only marvel at Spain's 'proper' high-speed

AVE network, which covers greater domestic distances (and some international routes – currently Barcelona to Lyon and Madrid to Marseille) at speeds of up to 310 km/h.

Stepping off the train in Cordoba, I had to think of one of my old comic annuals – probably *The Beezer* – that I used to get for Christmas in the 1970s. In those days, as well as featuring all your favourite cartoon characters, they included more educational features on historical themes, wildlife, and so on. I can remember one of them had a piece on Cordoba, illustrated with magical drawings of grand, golden buildings. And soon enough, there they were in front of us, coming to life after all those years. Saying it's an impressive city is like saying the Empire State Building is a bit tall. A day trip really wasn't enough to do justice to anything other than a quick taste of the highlights. We walked over the remarkable Roman Bridge dating from the first century B.C. and admired the views across to the golden, glowing old town. The remarkable remains of a Roman temple were a short walk away but the most imposing sights for me belonged to the city's Moorish past – the incredible Mosque Cathedral being the most famous. It is genuinely like nothing else I've ever seen. Once one of the most important mosques in the Islamic world, it was largely left intact when it was reclaimed by the Christians, who basically extended it with an equally immense and exuberant cathedral. The result is a colossal religious hybrid of an edifice, locked in its own internal 'look-at-me' competition. The mosque's candy cane forest of red and white arches sits alongside the elaborate ornamentation of the Catholic cathedral, creating a unique spectacle and a quite moving visual experience. If you didn't believe in God before you went in, you will by the time you come out.

After wandering around in awe, we ventured back outside for the more earthly delights of tapas and beer and then continued our sightseeing. Eventually, we found ourselves close to the station; the train we were booked on wouldn't leave for quite a while, but heading back into the centre wouldn't have really been worth it at that point, so we decided to see if our tickets could be used on an earlier return service. My few words of Spanish don't stretch to this kind of enquiry, so I started off by asking a RENFE customer service agent (in Spanish) if she spoke English. It turned out I'd stumbled across Spain's rudest person – and these are very rare in Spain, so I was really unlucky. She spat me a vicious 'no' and a stream of Spanish invective accompanied by a look of unadulterated disdain, the like of which I don't think I've ever seen in my life – luckily. As she got up and walked away, my jaw dropped at this unprovoked venomous display– anyone would have thought I'd dropped my trousers and asked for marks out of ten (I did look down briefly to check there was nothing awry). The man sitting at the desk next to her chipped in at this point, looking rather embarrassed, to ask how he could help. His advice was to ask at another office further along.

So, somewhat bemused, we headed off in search of the appropriate section. It really was an unfathomably odd reaction, all the more so from someone working in a customer service capacity in a tourist city, but I suppose none of us ever knows what's just happened in someone's life before we enter from stage left. And dealing with an ever-increasing conveyor belt of tourists must at some point take its toll on the local population, I imagine. Still pondering this, we walked along and soon spotted the 'correct' enquiries office. This time, there were three officials standing behind ticket windows, and surprisingly, there was no queue. But as I approached the counter, the three employees all frantically gesticulated that I needed to use the machine at the entrance. I tried arguing that I actually needed to speak to a human being... but the gesticulatory protests continued behind the glass. After surrendering and persevering a short while with said machine, I realised it would generate an enquiry number that was promptly printed off on a small square piece of paper. Once delivered, I extracted it from the machine, then watched as the same number miraculously appeared on the electronic display above the counters – at which point, I was invited forward. This seemed a bizarre and over-complicated mixture of old-tech and high-tech, but by this point I was losing the will to live. And after all this, it turned out our tickets weren't valid for any other train and couldn't be changed, so we went for a beer and waited. It was a slightly weird conclusion to what had otherwise been an absolutely glorious and memorable train trip to Cordoba; and that of course is what it's all about in the end.

Train travel thoughts M

Never under-estimate the emotional impact (good *and* bad) that travel can have on you.

Resist overwhelming folk with your travellers' tales on return; but don't be surprised if even the short version sometimes falls on deaf ears.

If you're doing a continuous journey over several days, make sure you've got sufficient supplies and take nothing for granted.

If you're travelling well off the beaten track, there's often something to be said for trying not to stand out, especially in potentially risky areas.

Always check in advance whether you need a visa, even if you're just passing through.

If you're heading somewhere to see a specific thing/sight, it's worth checking that it's still open.

Be sure to mind your Ps and Qs when dealing with railway customer services – if they actually let you speak to them.

N

N1 - Nice to Monte Carlo and Ventimiglia – on the TER (Transport Express Régional)

Route: Nice – Villefranche-sur-Mer – Beaulieu-sur-Mer – Eze – Monaco Monte Carlo – Menton - Ventimiglia

This was my first train trip abroad after Covid and the various lockdowns, so it was great to be away and back on a train, even if it was a fairly short journey. It was also our first time in Nice, and we loved it. The old town was predictably gorgeous, full of meandering Italianate alleyways, squares and cafes (Nice had in fact once belonged to Italy). We also did the compulsory strolling along the Promenade des Anglais (pictures of which I still remember seeing in French textbooks at school) and climbed up to the Colline du Chateau to see the amazing city panoramas and the elegantly imposing 'cascade' waterfall. It was up there that we almost died – there's a daily midday cannon blast which we didn't know about. When it went off VERY close by, I felt the blast reverberate in every fibre of my being. It was truly a sphincter-challenging moment. A more pleasant highlight was getting the bus up to the wonderfully refined Cimiez district and seeing where many Victorians (including the Queen herself) had once holidayed. How the other half live...

Although the train journey from Nice to Ventimiglia only

takes about fifty minutes, it's fairly remarkable in managing to pass through three countries in that amount of time – France, Monaco and Italy. The prospect of a journey along the French and Italian Riviera naturally conjures up thoughts of glitz and glamour. But in reality, the trip couldn't have been less glamorous. I'd read this particular stretch was often hellishly busy during the summer months. But since we were travelling in early June, I'd naively thought we'd be spared the worst, being just outside the peak tourist season. God only knows how bad it must be in July and August because this was a total trial. The frequency of services along the French Riviera is actually very good, with two or more trains covering the coastal stretch every hour. The problem is the sheer number of tourists in the area using them. The stretch is served by local trains which can't be booked in advance, as is the case in most countries. This means that at each stop, huge numbers of tourists cram themselves onto the trains, trying to get to the various other resorts along the coast – St Tropez, Cannes, Antibes, Eze, Menton and so on. There's a mass exodus at Nice but hundreds more take their place. No wonder the service has a reputation for being a pickpocket's paradise.

We'd travelled on the same service to Monte Carlo earlier that week (more on that shortly) and it had been like a phone box competition of old where people tried to break the record for the number of folk who can stuff themselves inside. The only good thing to say about that journey was that it was a short ride of about twenty minutes. There was a brief moment of hilarity (experienced only by me) when someone stood on David's flip-flop, removing it from his foot as we climbed to the upper deck (the train was a double-decker). Because it was so full and nobody could move, he was only able to retrieve the flip-flop by contorting himself like a disgruntled yoga master. Those nearby looked on in disdainful confusion and alarm, oblivious to the wandering flip-flop down below.

You'd think we might have known better when we decided to get back on board a few days later and travel on further to cross the Italian border. I always think it might be better next time... it wasn't. In fact, initially, it was far worse. As we stood on the platform in Nice awaiting the train with hordes of others, the first annoyance was an ever increasing delay. When it finally arrived, mass jostling ensued as the train doors opened. To everyone's astonishment, the sight that greeted them was the full phone-box competition view. Some brave and hardy souls did their best to re-enact David's flip-flop manoeuvre by inserting themselves between people's legs to scramble on board. I've got to the point now where I look defeat in the eye when I see it and leave it be. As disappointing – and sweltering – as it was on the platform, I know when I'm beaten. The doors closed again, and off it went, carrying the crammed, sweating masses with it.

Not two minutes later, however, things were suddenly looking up – French Railways, aware of the chaos, decided to put on an extra train – and there it suddenly was! Empty and waiting. Hats off to SNCF for stepping in and taking such prompt action. Within minutes we were on board, seated and settled, and not a single crotch or elbow thrust in our faces. It's funny how small wins like this are a massive source of elation – for me at any rate. After what looked like a journey written off, we were now sitting comfortably and enjoying the views – and what views they are – sublime. The train hugs the coast most of the way, offering breathtaking views of blue sea, enchanting bays, picturesque medieval towns and more – simply cinematic. Things change briefly once the train pulls into Monte Carlo station – quite a remarkable and surprisingly huge station (for the size of the place), cut into the mountain rock. In fact, it feels and looks more like the underground lair of a Bond villain than a railway station.

As mentioned, we'd visited Monaco a couple of days prior to this trip, and trying to find an exit from the station on arrival only made it feel more like the den of a super villain. Following the exit signs offered no reassurance whatsoever – walking along enormous passageways, going up stairs, coming back down escalators, more passageways, then up in a lift. Surely this couldn't be right? Was this part of somebody's evil plan to keep us down there forever, as they watched the ridiculous spectacle on CCTV, giggling diabolically? Eventually, we emerged outside, but I have no idea how.

Once outside, I'm still not entirely sure what to make of Monte Carlo. The location between the hills and the sea is admittedly stunning, especially on a glorious summer's day. As you'd expect, everything about the place oozes wealth, style and luxury, but it's another of those cities that has the effect of worzel-gummidgizing me – I walk round feeling totally out of place, waiting to be arrested by the fashion police. Never more so than when walking around the famous Monte Carlo Casino, where I felt obliged to preface every sentence with the words, 'So, Mr Bond...' which I appreciate must get annoying after an hour or two. There's certainly no doubting it's a playground for the rich and famous; the price of a couple of beers outside the casino made that abundantly clear. And then there's the men walking around in super stylish suits and sunglasses, bronzed and elegant, and the ladies walking their tiny little dogs, dressed like Audrey Hepburn in a 50s film. It's all very impressive but quite unreal somehow. In fact, it all had the distancing effect of making me feel I could only ever be an observer here – this wasn't a world I'd ever be given permanent admission to.

We decided to reduce the all-encroaching and oppressive glamour by getting on the public bus up to Monaco City, the old part of town. This was definitely more my thing – narrow winding streets, stately stone buildings that offered some shade and a sense of history. Like most people, I'm sure, I tried to imagine Grace Kelly walking in and around the grounds of the Prince's Palace, looking down on the phenomenal view of Monte Carlo harbour and the hundreds of yachts moored there. In a nutshell, it was all impressively beautiful but just a bit too much, and though I'd enjoyed the day we spent there, I wasn't sorry when we headed back to the station to spend another hour working out how to re-penetrate the railway cavern and find the train back to Nice. This all went through my mind again while the train waited on the platform in Monte Carlo. Seemingly hundreds of people got off, and even more tried to get on. After a short while, we were moving again and the train emerged from the mountain, back into France, and the breathtaking views resumed. A short time later, after seriously impressive views of Menton old town, we entered Italy, and a short time after that, the train pulled into the Italian border town of Ventimiglia.

Not many people these days have heard of Ventimiglia. Admittedly, it's a relatively small town in a country chock full of impressive towns and cities. That said, its station is huge, partly because of its status as a border town. In the past, this made it the destination for a huge number of long distance international services from elsewhere in Europe. Up until the early 1990s (yet again) there were direct services from as far away as Hamburg, Vienna and Venice. Of particular note is the remarkable Flanders

Riviera Express. This train was an amazing collection of through coaches from Amsterdam, Brussels, Lille and Calais that met in Paris for their onward overnight journey to Marseille, Nice and, finally, Ventimiglia. A version managed to survive between Lille and Nice until 2009, by which time the Amsterdam-Ventimiglia connection had long since disappeared. There was also the famously evocative Blue Train (so named because of its dark blue sleeping cars) that ran for many years from Paris to Ventimiglia. This train had run since 1920, originally as a luxury CIWL service and at times had through coaches from Calais, but by 2003, it too was consigned to history.

Ventimiglia is still a very charming small town on the Italian Riviera. Most people travel on through to Milan and Genoa but it is worth a visit, with its charmingly ramshackle old town high up above the Roya River and the more modern but pretty commercial centre close to the station and beach. As we walked around, it was impossible not to notice the large numbers of African and Middle Eastern migrants who'd clearly got stuck there as they struggled to continue their onward journeys to France, Britain and other destinations in Northern Europe. Migration is of course a difficult and controversial matter that many countries are currently struggling with and, though people's views differ, it's hard not to be moved by the sight of people sleeping rough in railway sidings, looking undernourished and frankly desperate. On the train back we were alarmed to hear squealing and shouting shortly after arriving at Menton Gavarin, the first station in France after the Italian border. Looking out of the window, we saw French border police manhandling two African women onto the platform. They were clearly distressed and it was upsetting to see people being treated so roughly. They were escorted away, so I have no idea what happened next. Suddenly, my moaning about packed trains felt very self-indulgent, and the opulence of the French Riviera sat rather uncomfortably alongside the obvious plight of individuals searching for a better life.

N2 - New York to Poughkeepsie – on the Hudson (River) Line

Route: New York Grand Central – Harlem – Tarrytown – Croton-Harmon – Peekskill – Garrison – Cold Spring – New Hamburg – Poughkeepsie

This is the only train trip I've ever been on in the USA. At about 100 km and taking over two hours, it's not exactly a ride on the Twentieth Century Limited (New York to Chicago) or the Super Chief (Chicago to Los Angeles) but it still felt like a real adventure and I loved every minute of it. I'd turned fifty earlier that year and, like most people, I wanted to do something special to mark it when the summer holiday came round. A trip to New York had been on the bucket list for some time, so hitting fifty seemed a good time to get it ticked off.

I'm sure New York is one of those places that people either love or hate; in my case, I absolutely loved it – it's mad, sophisticated, depressing, exciting, huge and a million-and-one other contradictory things - but I found it completely absorbing. If I'm honest, part of my fascination comes from seeing it (as so many of us have done) in umpteen films over the years, and some of my favourite ones at that – *Midnight Cowboy, King Kong, Rosemary's Baby, Saturday Night Fever, Eyes Wide Shut, Working Girl*... the list is endless, and I won't even mention the TV programmes we all know that it's featured in. Consequently, it's hard not to feel we know it and, in a small way, I suppose we do, after years of regular TV exposure. So seeing the various sights and connecting back to all sorts of memories was inevitable and strangely moving at times – walking out of the lift on top of the Empire State Building, for example, how could I not think of the first time I stayed up late to watch King Kong frightening the life out of Faye Wray up there, sitting at home with my dad for the regular Saturday night BBC2 horror double bill?

But enough of TV memory lane. After a week of taking in the sights, walking our legs off and re-mortgaging the house every time we stopped for a drink, we decided to take the train to upstate New York to have a more leisurely week exploring the beautiful countryside in the Catskills. The journey started with a walk down to Grand Central Station. Yet again, it's hard to believe you haven't stepped onto a film set — we've all seen it in so many films, and suddenly there it is and you're in the middle of it! It absolutely lives up to the grand in its name. It's an immense, golden-glowing cathedral of a station, right up there for me with Milan and Antwerp. Standing at the ticket window felt again like recreating so many TV scenes and it made me wonder if this would ever start to feel commonplace if you actually lived there. We bought two tickets for Poughkeepsie (pronounced Pukipsee) and headed for the platform — a much darker and dingier Gotham-looking section of the station that put me in mind of films where people get pushed onto the tracks by homicidal maniacs.

The train we were getting was operated by Metro North Railroad and would run the whole length of the Hudson (River) Line (you may have guessed it, it was impossible not to be humming Billy Joel, even if he was taking a Greyhound). We were soon seated (even if the seats were a little firm and unforgiving) and moving northwards out of the station into New York's iconic cityscape. I'm not sure if it's a bit pathetic for a man of fifty to feel so excited about a train ride but I think we probably have to try and stop caring what other people might think about us after a certain age. We pushed on up through Manhattan and, after a short stop in Harlem, it was on through the Bronx and Yonkers, after which the urban sprawl gradually began to thin and the countryside reclaimed the views as we travelled along the eastern shore of the Hudson River.

As the river widened and we moved further into the Hudson Highlands, the scenery improved by the mile. Gentle hills, the meandering river, lush greenery – ok, it wasn't the Alps, but it was lovely. After a few stops we reached the small town of Garrison. Lots of military personnel got on at this point (I suppose the clue is in the name); it turns out that the West Point Military Academy was based close by. The only other thing I knew about Garrison before that was that it had been used as a set stand-in for Yonkers in the 1969 Barbra Streisand film, *Hello Dolly*. There didn't appear to be any obvious lasting legacy from this involvement, as far as I could establish from the train.

Barbra Streisand or no Barbra Streisand, the train ambled along and more green forests and rolling hills passed by. After about two hours, we reached our destination of Poughkeepsie, the 'Queen of the Hudson,' and a town that had once been New York's state capital. The human scale and small city feel was a welcome breather after the full-on sensory overload of New York. We walked around the old historic centre and relaxed in the bars and restaurants that were clustered down by the Hudson. I was a bit surprised at one point to be asked "if you guys are from some foreign country or something?" But then maybe they don't get to hear many English Midlands accents 'in them there parts'. The next step further on into the Catskills meant hiring a car, as Poughkeepsie was the end of the Metro North train line. We could have taken other trains heading up to Niagara Falls and even Toronto on the Empire Line... but they'll maybe have to wait for another landmark birthday.

Train travel thoughts N

Some routes are really best only travelled in winter and autumn – once again, a bit of research before you go is never a bad thing; and sometimes, bus services can be a better bet/less manic than the train.

Once again, money belts are a good investment if you know you're doing a journey where it's likely to be standing room only, especially in busy tourist spots.

Do ten weeks' overtime before you go to New York; you'll need it to afford the exorbitant tips alone.

O

O - Ostend to Warsaw – back on the Ost West Express

Route: Ostend – Bruges – Ghent – Brussels – Liège – Aachen – Cologne – Dusseldorf – Dortmund – Hanover – Berlin Schönefeld Airport – Frankfurt/Oder – Kunowice – Poznan - Warsaw

This was another journey on the East West Express and although this one was from west to east, the train's name never changed. The Ost West Express (as it was featured in most European timetables) was for many years – as the name implies – one of the principal trains connecting Eastern and Western Europe. As mentioned earlier, it was another good example of complex rail manoeuvres that saw through coaches added and detached at various stations across the Continent. It ran for several decades from the 1950s, and finally disappeared from the timetables in 1998, when it was replaced by the shorter EuroNight Jan Kiepura service (Brussels – Warsaw).

Before then, its main route had been from Paris (later on Brussels) to Moscow via Berlin, Warsaw and Minsk. As stated, not all of its carriages travelled the entire route. Through coaches from the Hook of Holland and Ostend enabled passengers to and from the UK (as well as Dutch and Belgian travellers) to pick up this direct connection to Moscow and for a time there was even a direct sleeping car between Brussels and Saint Petersburg. Because the train's carriages were provided by numerous railway companies, it was often a very colourful sight, with Russian sleepers, East and West German carriages, Polish and Danish couchette cars and so on. This made walking through the train quite an experience in itself, given the various nationalities on board and the signs on display in Russian, Polish, German and other languages. I'll never forget the smell of the former East German (DR) carriages – they used a very distinctive disinfectant as part of their cleaning regime which meant their carriages were immediately identifiable by an overpowering smell that hit the back of your throat like a swig of meths. I've got some old East German train signs in my collection, and even after forty years my cupboards still stink of them – powerful stuff.

This particular journey was yet another of our early 1990s trips, and getting off the ferry and walking onto the station concourse in Ostend was still a magical moment for me, seeing the various trains waiting to depart to all parts of the Continent. Since the launch of Eurostar, Ostend – and for that matter Calais and the Hook of Holland – are stations very few UK visitors ever set foot in any more. But pre-Chunnel, they were still the Continental points of entry for all those travelling by rail and sea from Britain. This had in fact been the case since the 19th Century, when train travel was *the* way to travel abroad and, as such, these three stations in particular were of longstanding significance for British travellers. It's worth dwelling on this for a moment to show just how important Ostend was for train travellers back in the day. To illustrate this, here's a table showing the range and number of direct rail destinations still available from Ostend in the 1980s, many of which survived into the 90s:

Austria	Innsbruck, Vienna (Ostend Vienna Express/Donauwalzer/Austria Nacht Express), Graz, Klagenfurt (Tauern Express), Salzburg, Zell am See, Villach, Landeck
Belgium	Bruges, Ghent, Brussels, Antwerp, Liège, etc
Denmark	Copenhagen (Nord Express)
France	Cerbère, Narbonne, La Tour de Carol, St. Raphael-Valescure
Germany	Aachen, Cologne, Dortmund, Frankfurt (Memling), Hamburg, Hanover, Berlin, Munich (Bayern Nacht Express)
Italy	Bolzano, Merano, Milan, Ancona, Rome (Freccia del Tirreno), Verona
Luxembourg	Luxembourg Ville

Poland	Poznan, Warsaw (Ost West Express)
Russia	Smolensk, Moscow (Ost West Express)
Switzerland	Basle, Zurich, Chur, Brig, Chiasso, Sierre
Yugoslavia	Ljubljana, Zagreb, Split (Tauern Express)

Some of these trains had been running with the same name for over a hundred years by this point (e.g. the Ostend Vienna Express, the Nord Express to Copenhagen, etc.) while others ran under new names, like the Bavaria Night Express to Munich and the Freccia del Tirreno to Rome.

Surveying the departure board, we soon found our way to the platform where the East West Express was waiting. We still had quite a while before it left at 17.34, so I nipped across to a supermarket just outside the station to stock up on a few provisions. Again, there was minimal catering available on the train and it'd be 12.30 the next day before we got to Warsaw. We'd splashed out and reserved a sleeping compartment for the two of us but, unfortunately, this meant we were booked into the Russian sleeping car – an old Soviet carriage that had definitely seen better days (though God knows quite when). It was dark and dingy, and gave the impression of stepping forty years back in time. Things didn't improve any when Margaret spotted squashed fleas on the supposedly 'fresh' bedding supplied. The fleas were at least dead but I'm not sure that lifted the vibe at all. I had a word with the provodnik to see if there was a chance of an upgrade of any sort, but as I suspected, the answer was a firmly dismissive 'nyet'. Russian customer service in those days still seemed in its infancy, if this particular attendant was anything to go by (an impression later reinforced by our entire stay in the country). She patrolled the carriage with the warmth of a prison guard, scowling severely on each interaction. When I had asked her for two teas, I'd stated 'No sugar' very clearly in Russian but, as she handed me the drinks, I could see each glass of tea had a good inch of standing sugar in the bottom. I reminded her that I had said 'without sugar'.... her reply was simple but stern: "Don't stir!"

The next carriage along was a Polish couchette car going as far as Warsaw – swish, modern, clean and looked after by a cheerful Pole who said we could happily take a couple of spare berths in one of the compartments. We did consider it but it would have meant sharing with four others after shelling out quite a sum for our own two-berth compartment. In the end, we made the best of it and reminded ourselves that the fleas were dead – we just hoped they didn't have any living relatives. Before too much longer we were well on our way through Flanders, feeling a little more mellow as we watched the gentle scenery passing by. By the time we got to Brussels and had opened the wine, the grot didn't really seem that big a deal, and once we'd crossed into Germany and reached Cologne around 22.00, it was time to get the bedding sorted out and try and get some sleep for the night.

A fairly decent night followed, until the inevitable banging on the compartment door sometime after 5.00 the next morning – East German and Polish customs/border guards doing their routine inspections. It always feels very odd to me, dealing with uniformed officialdom at an unearthly hour while lying there unkempt, half naked and bleary-eyed, but all just in a day's work for them, I suppose. After that, there was still plenty of time to try for a bit more shut-eye before breakfast and a few more hours watching flat green fields pass by until midday and our arrival in the wonderful Polish capital, some nineteen hours after we'd left Ostend.

Marek was waiting for us on the platform at Warsaw Central, a 'modern' station that was built mid-1970s to showcase the power of the Polish People's Republic. This meant it was fairly austere and concrete-centric, but still compared quite favourably to Birmingham New Street at the time. Warsaw itself really grew on me in the few days we spent there. Admittedly, it's no Venice or Salzburg; but then it'd been knocked about quite a bit over the years, not least of all by the Nazis (putting it mildly; we'd walked around part of what had been the Warsaw ghetto

– Marek pointed out bullet indentations that were still visible). The Communists hadn't done much to lift the aesthetics either. But the sheer amount of restoration work that had been carried out in the few years since the fall of Communism was impressive and you had to admire the Poles' spirit and resolve. Though the soviet Palace of Culture and Science (Marek called it the 'wedding cake' and said it was an unwanted 'gift' from Stalin) still dominates the centre, the old quarters have been painstakingly reconstructed to wonderful effect, especially around the main Market Square. I've been back a few times since then and it's marvellous to see how it's flourished and reclaimed much of its former glory.

Though the direct connection from Ostend is now long gone, reaching Warsaw by train is probably easier than ever before, with various options available. The easiest is probably an afternoon Eurostar to Brussels where you can pick up the night train to Berlin (currently, Nightjet and European Sleeper both run services on the route). Once in Berlin, there are multiple fast trains each day to Warsaw – and not a dead flea to be found anywhere, I'm sure!

Train travel thoughts O

Stuck record time – make sure you've got something to eat and drink if you're travelling overnight, despite what might be stated in any on or offline blurb.

The standard of overnight accommodation has vastly improved right across Europe these days but, if you do have an issue, it's always worth asking the attendant, even if you do get a 'nyet'.

P

P1 - Prague to Krakow – on the Silesia Express

Route: Prague – Kolin – Pardubice – Olomouc – Ostrava – Petrovice u Karvine – Zebrzydowice – Auschwitz - Krakow

It's difficult not to fall in love with Prague, as anyone who's ever been there will tell you – and plenty of people have certainly been there. The city is yet another European hotspot currently struggling with overtourism. Apparently, it has eight times more tourists than residents – a frightening ratio, and small wonder there are reports of increasing tensions between locals and visitors, many of whom are not always on their best behaviour, especially the stag and hen do crowd...But back in the 1990s, the time of my last visit, it was busy but more than bearable, though the usual crowds gathered in front of the medieval Astronomical Clock and strolled over Charles Bridge. Let's face it, the city was not at the back of the queue when prizes for gorgeousness were being handed out. And what an eclectic set of beautiful features it has – if it's not Baroque, it's Gothic; if not Art Nouveau, it's Romanesque. And all stunningly put together in a way that makes you want to wander around forever, trapped in its photogenic splendour. And maybe that's why it is so much busier these days – perhaps people never do leave, they just get joined by more.

I was certainly happy to have another full day to explore before heading off, this time on a night train to Krakow, the Silesia Express. This particular train still runs to this day (at the time of writing) though as an EC day train, along with two others - the EC Cracovia and a privately run Leo Express. The current night train is the EN Chopin service. Back in the mid-1990s I was still trying to travel cheap, so I'd taken the chance of not booking a sleeper or couchette in the hope that it wouldn't be busy and I could sleep on a row of seats. As it turned out, luck was on my side for once and I found an empty compartment. The train had carriages bound for Warsaw as well as Krakow, so I just had to make sure I was in a carriage that would be uncoupled at the border and head off in the right direction, i.e. to Krakow. Just before the train left at around 21.30, I was joined by Ken, an American student from Indiana. Two people in a compartment for six was still a win in my book, and after a few days of travelling alone, it was nice to have some company and a few beers.

This was Ken's first trip to Europe and Prague had been his chosen first destination. He seemed a little nervous about everything – so much so, in fact, I was surprised he'd decided to travel overnight by train. This was also his first experience of a night train, and he spent ages trying to work out if he could somehow lock the door. As it was a seating compartment, this option didn't exist, a conclusion he was eventually forced to accept with some disquiet, despite trying to wedge his rucksack against the handle in all sorts of ingenious but futile ways. I tried to reassure him that we were safe but didn't get the impression I was succeeding. When the conductor opened the door for a ticket inspection, Ken was in full panic mode – 'What the hell is this guy saying, what does he want??' Again, I reassured him it was just a routine ticket inspection.

After a while, I popped to the toilet at the end of the carriage and noticed the train destination sign which listed the various stops on the way to Krakow. It was strange seeing Auschwitz as one of the stops, or at least the modern town of Oświęcim as it's called in Polish. I mentioned this to Ken when I was back in the compartment – this seemed to unsettle him considerably. I must admit it did feel strange, the thought of being on a night train passing through Auschwitz. It was difficult not to consider the horror of people in far less fortunate circumstances making this journey during the war – truly horrendous, and a chill certainly ran down my spine. But Ken seemed deeply shocked and disturbed and reached for another beer. We chatted about our lives, the way you sometimes do with total strangers and, after a time, the effects of beer plus days of travelling and sightseeing took their toll, so we decided it was time to bed down. Again, it was good to have the compartment to ourselves and to be able to lie down on the seats for the night.

Before long I nodded off. I'd been pleasantly surprised

that the train wasn't too busy, and that had so far made for a peaceful journey. Sometime after passing through Ostrava in the east of the Czech Republic, the train stopped in the border town of Petrovice u Karviné. I only remember this because of what always happens on night trains at borders – at least in the pre-Schengen days – the border guards come a-knocking. On this particular night, they weren't exactly being shy about popping by – they hammered heavily on the door, swung it open, and said something loud in Czech or Polish which had the word 'pasportny' (or something similar) in the middle of it. I was duly reaching for my money belt to present said item, when Ken suddenly gasped in absolute horror, 'Oh my God, who are these guys now and what do they want??' Once again, I reassured him this was just a routine border inspection and all part of normal procedure. He didn't exactly help himself by not being willing to let them handle his passport – he opened it at the picture page but kept it in his hands. They, of course, wanted to get their hands on it for the full official flick-through, which Ken tried to resist, not doing himself any favours in the process. This led to a very odd passport tug-of-war scenario, Ken still fully resisting.

In the end, the border guards naturally won, and to make a point, decided on a full and vigorous luggage inspection – all items taken out of his rucksack, felt, fumbled and fiddled with, Ken mumbling the whole time about rights' violations and such like – all of which fell on deaf

Czech/Polish ears. Eventually, they moved on further down the carriage and the train continued into the Polish night. We arrived in Krakow a little bleary-eyed at around 6.00 the next morning and said our goodbyes on the station platform. I headed off to meet my Polish friend, Marek; Ken headed off to get something for his nerves, no doubt. I've sometimes wondered how he coped with the rest of his trip – and his life, for that matter; for me, these mini-encounters are one of the poignant pleasures of travelling long distances by train – the short but memorable crossings of lives, of people whom we, in most cases, will never ever meet again, but who stay with us as stories.

P2 – Porto to Pinhão – on an interregional train along the Douro Valley

Route: Porto - Ermesinde – Paredes – Marco de Canaveses – Aregos – Regua – Ferrao – Pinhão

David and I were having a week's break in Porto and had heard wonderful things about the Douro Valley. From what we'd been told, the train seemed to be one of the best ways to see it (outside of a river cruise) so that sounded just the job. We were staying in the city centre so started out from Porto's Sao Bento station, the terminus of the city's principal suburban lines. I'd seen it countless times on TV as it's been featured in no end of travel programmes. The entrance hall to the station is the big attraction – around 20,000 blue azulejo tiles were used to create murals on the surrounding walls, and what a magnificent sight they are. I'd wondered again whether reality would match up to the TV hype, but it was nothing short of extraordinary. And this was just walking into the station! After several minutes craning our necks and admiring the incredible workmanship, we bought our tickets and jumped onto a local train heading to Porto's main railway station, Porto Campanha.

This station was a far more prosaic looking job but it was here we could pick up the Douro Valley line. From various conversations we'd had, and also my bit of online research, the suggestion was that the small town of Pinhão was a good place to head to. At around two-and-a-half hours each way, this seemed like plenty of time for a day trip, allowing for a wander round and a bite to eat once we got there. I was tempted to get tickets to Pocinho, a further hour away; word had it that the views were even more amazing on the stretch between Pinhão and Pocinho, but a seven hour round trip seemed a bit daunting, the more so as I was coming down with a tedious cold and not feeling at my best – typical, of course, but Pinhão seemed like a sensible compromise under the circumstances.

Soon enough, we pulled out of Campanha station, and before long we were travelling along the Douro Valley, the meandering river on our right hand side, with beautiful views of lush, terraced vineyards climbing up from the lower banks. And so it continued, the glorious summer weather providing a wonderful backdrop and making me ask myself why I didn't live there. I wonder if people who live in picturesque places like this ever grow tired of being surrounded by such constant beauty? Pondering this brought *Adrian Mole* to mind – in Sue Townsend's wonderful *Growing Pains*, she has Adrian writing a novel about a suave sophisticate whose words suggest that this is perhaps eventually the case:

> "Jason Westmoreland's copper-flecked eyes glanced cynically around the terrace. He was sick of Capri and longed for Wolverhampton."

Maybe it'd take quite a long time to get to that point and, sitting on the train taking in the breathtaking beauty, I certainly wasn't anywhere near there yet. The only slight niggle was the smell – the regional train we were on was a diesel, and the smell of the fumes coming in was quite overwhelming at times. I'm not sure why it was quite so bad, as I've been on plenty of diesel trains over the years and this was the only time it felt like I'd got my nose hooked up to a diesel inhaler. That and the nicely developing runny nose were a bit of a pain, but then I suppose it was at least saving me from being overwhelmed by unadulterated pleasure; who knows, I might have gone mad with ecstasy otherwise.

125 km and endless expanses of gorgeous greenery later, the train stopped in Pinhão, where we jumped off into the burning heat of the early afternoon sun. Its little

country station is a gem in itself and, though not on the same scale as Sao Bento station, still beautifully decorated with blue and white tiles. The town is situated just at the confluence of the Douro and Pinhão Rivers which makes for further spectacular views all around. We were keen to stretch our legs and get something to eat (not at the same time) so, after a quick mosey about, we headed into the shade of a cafe with an outdoor terrace (and parasols). A few beers and a hefty lunch later, we were back on our feet, dodging the harsh sun as much as possible, and on our way back to the station.

Even though we were retracing the same route on the way back, the change in direction and angle of the sun presented a different but equally lovely perspective on the valley; however, it still felt like I was sucking on a diesel pipe for the duration. I think I nodded off for a while in the warmth, the cold also progressing to the heavy head stage by this point. The two or so hours sped by, and we were soon back at Sao Bento station, admiring its amazingly tiled hall for the last time. As for Porto itself – it's a city I'd go back to in a heartbeat. The home of port, and another UNESCO World Heritage Site, it's beautifully located on the Douro Estuary. And although it's quite a big city, it manages to retain a kind of small-town charm. The colourful, terraced rows of buildings viewed from across the river are dazzling, and the waterside cafes and restaurants are marvellous places to relax and people watch. It may have lost its direct connection to Paris with the demise of the Sud Express (see Y below), but that's probably about the only thing it has lost.

Train travel thoughts P

It's rarely a good idea to get bolshy with border guards.

If you can, lock your compartment door when you're travelling overnight, but don't get paranoid if you can't. Again, just make sure the important stuff is in your money belt.

Always have some cold and flu remedies/paracetamol with you.

Q

Q - Moscow to Vologda – on the Archangel Express

Route: Moscow Yaroslavskaya – Rostov – Yaroslavl – Danilov - Vologda

Ok, so I can guess what you're thinking now – how does this journey fall under Q? It's a fair question. The simple answer is that I don't think I've ever been anywhere beginning with a Q, let alone travelled from there by train. I can only think of Quimper, Quebec and Quezon City, and probably quite a few places in China, but again, I've never been. So from an A-Z point-of-view, I'm taking a bit of a liberty. I respectfully crave your indulgence, dear reader. That said, there is one very good reason the above journey sort of does fall under Q – getting on this train involved joining the biggest QUEUE I've ever been in in my entire life, and that's genuinely no exaggeration. I'll explain why.

This was another leg on our Russian train travels thirty years ago. After several days in Moscow, we were travelling 500 km north east to a city called Vologda where we'd arranged to spend a week or more staying with a local family. Very generously, the family's teenage son, Dimitri, had met us in Moscow and organised our tickets up to Vologda, so all we had to do was follow our guide and enjoy the ride. The train was leaving from Moscow's Yaroslavskaya Station (every station we'd seen in Moscow was immense) and was bound for the Arctic city of Archangel (Arkhangelsk), about 1300 km north of Moscow. Yet again, we were on a night train, leaving at around 22.00.

We headed to the platform, and what a sight it was – a huge, milling mass of people. Now I'm no stranger to busy platforms – like many of us, I've stood on them at Birmingham New Street and London Euston at peak times, jostling for a space and place with the best of them, but this was in another league altogether. It was as if Wembley Stadium had been emptied at high speed and funnelled onto the platform. To add to the sense of manic mayhem, lots of the waiting passengers looked as if they were going in for some sort of 'who can amass the most stuff to lug' competition – there were umpteen buckets of vegetables, clucking chickens in cardboard boxes wrapped in string, prams, furniture, and – no joke – someone actually with a kitchen sink (well, a small hand basin). This is to say nothing of children, babies, rucksacks, pets and everything else you'd expect. Dimitri said this was the time of year when lots of people were returning home from Georgia, where things were far more plentiful; seeing the general deprivation in Vologda later on, we totally understood why.

Right on time, the Archangel Express pulled in and it had to be the longest train I have ever seen – carriage after carriage after carriage sidling along the platform and gradually grinding to a slow halt. As always happens, most people were not standing by the carriage they were booked onto – cue mass shuffling on a scale I have never before witnessed. Margaret looked very close to tears, and I must admit, if I wasn't so macho (ahem) I could have easily started blubbing. We were tossed around in this colossal maelstrom of folk moving themselves and their chattels up and down the platform. Looking back now, it's the sort of experience some people would probably pay for these days at Drayton Manor Park or Alton Towers, if the event ever got signed off by the health and safety authorities. It truly was an overwhelming physical and mental experience, and still to this day I have no idea how we ever got through this immense and chaotic queue to the correct carriage and managed to board the train. I can only think Dimitri must have miraculously guided us through it all and finally got us to our berths.

Once we were on board, it carried on in much the same vein. To add to the strangeness of it all, Dimitri told us not to speak under any circumstances... we asked why but got no answer; this was only just post-Soviet Russia, so we thought it best to ask later and treat it like a sponsored silence in the meantime. This would also be our first encounter with the Russian concept of travelling 'platzkart'. We'd never heard of this, let alone seen anything like it. In a nutshell, the carriage was a kind of Soviet-style dormitory sleeping car – if you can imagine over fifty berths filling the carriage and corridor, with a slim walkway through, but no partitions or curtains, with all the allure of sleeping on a supermarket shelf. By the time everybody had established they were in the right carriage, the mass jostling continued for the right berth. Eventually, of course, we found ours and flung ourselves (silently) onto them.

I will never forget lying down, catching my breath, then staring across and seeing an elderly woman opposite smiling at me as she cuddled her chicken (not a euphemism). I should also mention that it was hot – VERY hot. This was August and there was no doubting it. As I lay there, it really felt as if I'd lain down fully clothed in a sauna – and a sauna filled with all the farmyard fun your nostrils could cope with. At moments like these, I find you just have to embrace defeat again. You're hot, soaked with sweat (not all of it your own), uncomfortable, confined and claustrophobic, but it ain't gonna change – not for nine hours, anyway. Accept it, deal with it and know it will end at some point.... if you don't first. Not the ideal recipe for a relaxing journey, let alone a good night's sleep, but we later learned that travelling this way was also three times cheaper (unsurprisingly). I won't mention the toilets because ... well, I won't mention the toilets.

I gather that platzkart travel still exists in Russia, with appropriate modern comfort upgrades, and I can see there are potential benefits once you know what you're letting yourself in for. It's certainly cheap, a good way to meet people and clearly a very sociable experience (if you're allowed to talk). I'd also imagine that the mass surveillance element means it's pretty safe – everyone can see what's happening and it'd be difficult for thieves or worse to get away with anything. That said, it's not an experience I'd rush to repeat but I suppose it does remind me that even in life's most trying times, it's good to know that 'this too will end'. The imposed silence turned out to be because of the tickets – at that time, there were still different prices for foreigners and Russian natives. Dimitri had bought three cheaper tickets for Russians only, so the idea was to not give the game away. Shame we didn't know while we were travelling – it would have added that last bit of stress and tension we were missing.

The rigours of the journey were soon forgotten once we arrived in Vologda. Like many places in Russia in the early 1990s, it was badly in need of some TLC and attention, but its charms were still obvious and many – its beautiful Kremlin and bell tower, the St. Sophia Cathedral and the Spaso-Prilutsky Monastery, to name but a few. There were some lovely walks down by the riverside, with wonderful views of the Kremlin and the old city centre. Signs of longstanding Soviet neglect were everywhere and at times overwhelming, and the family we stayed with needed to be incredibly resourceful and resilient to survive. Like many Russians, growing your own food was a practical necessity. I'll never forget walking around the city one day, and seeing dilapidated shop after shop that had completely run out of provisions to sell; the local post office didn't even have any stamps we could buy for a postcard home. The word was that supplies might be delivered at some point, but nobody seemed to know when. And from what we gathered, the locals had long been beaten into a subdued acceptance of these conditions; the east-west divide was still a startlingly dramatic contrast. I've not been back to Vologda since then, but looking online and seeing how it is now, things have clearly moved forward, and I hope that they can continue to.

Train travel thoughts Q

Always check to see if there's a carriage indicator on the train platform. If there is, it'll give you an idea of whereabouts to wait, and potentially minimise subsequent kerfuffle.

If you're having a rough old journey that there's no getting out of, muster as much zen as you can manage; and remember that it will end at some point, leaving you most likely with a tale to tell.

R

R1 - Ruse to Varna – on a Bulgarian intercity following the early Orient Express

Route: Ruse – Vetovo – Razgrad – Kaspichan – Dobrina – Sindel - Varna

In the late 1990s, I was working at a college in the West Midlands that was involved in a European project with three other countries – France, Germany and Bulgaria. I've met people who've been very dismissive about the value of such collaborations. I don't doubt that some such ventures might have been badly managed or of questionable worth, depending on how things are judged but my own experience of this particular science-related project was that it was of real benefit to the teenagers involved. The English students were 'ordinary' teenagers from various parts of the Black Country; many of them hadn't had an opportunity to travel abroad before, let alone work with students from other countries on shared curricular interests. Things like this will never be everybody's cup of tea but, for lots of the students, their involvement seemed like a really positive thing. It opened their eyes to different cultures, made them more curious and confident, deepened their interests in science and travel, developed their social skills... and in the process, they had a really enjoyable time of it too – how bad could that be?

The Bulgarian colleagues hosting us were based in the city of Ruse, the country's fifth largest city, located on the Danube opposite the Romanian town of Giurgiu. We'd flown to Sofia and then travelled up by coach to the northern border territory. Ruse itself was an interesting and handsome city, having at different times been under Roman, Ottoman and Communist rule, so a chequered past by anyone's standards, and history had certainly left its marks on the place. The return flight had been arranged from the city of Varna, just under 200 km away. As such, it was a fair bit closer than Sofia, and was easily accessible by rail from Ruse. I was delighted we had an opportunity to go there. As mentioned earlier, I've had a lifelong interest in Dracula (don't judge me) and, as any vampire aficionados will tell you, Varna is the Black Sea port that Dracula sets sail from after leaving Transylvania bound for Whitby. I was really looking forward to walking around the town and recapturing a sense of the Victorian vampire at large (I know, I know).

My other interest in travelling this route was historical and had to do with the Orient Express. When it was first launched in 1883, the 'Grand Express d'Orient', as it was known for the first eight years of its life, wasn't actually able to cover the whole distance to Istanbul, or Constantinople as it was then called. Travellers from Paris journeyed via Munich, Vienna, Budapest and Bucharest as far as Giurgiu on the opposite side of the Danube. Once at Giurgiu, passengers were ferried across to Ruse, where a train took them on to Varna for the final part of the 300 km journey by steamship across the Black Sea. The Ruse to Varna stretch apparently had a reputation for being the wildest section covered by the Orient Express, with bandits occasionally attacking the train – and even certain stations - on its way across the dusty landscape that hadn't much changed since medieval times, barring the odd Ottoman mosque and minaret on the horizon. And, taking things back to Dracula for a moment, Bram Stoker's book actually sees the count's destroyers travelling on the train from Paris to Varna on their final stake-out (weak pun intended).

But back to the late 1990s; at around four hours, the 200 km journey to Varna was still a relatively long one, especially considering this was billed as a fast train, but that didn't trouble me. The train itself looked like it dated back to Bulgaria's communist days. It was basic, old, clean enough and had no air conditioning, but the windows opened, so that wasn't an issue. On the plus side, it was spacious and not too busy, so there was plenty of room to stretch my legs. As Ruse is a border station, it was all go outside on the station platform. I noticed a train from Bucharest to Thessaloniki had stopped on the opposite platform, and watched as beggars trailed the length and breadth of the train, knocking on open windows, hoping, I supposed, to engage passengers and get a few coins or notes. Others walked up and down with fruit and bottles of water, trying to make a bit of cash by selling a few provisions. This must have been quite a decent business, I'd imagine, as not many of these international express trains provided catering, so this was often a handy and welcome service for many passengers. Some of the beggars looked like very sorry souls, to say the least, whilst others looked a little menacing and very unwashed. Even though this was a hundred years later, it may not have been that much different here in those very early days of the Orient Express.

Once we set off for Varna, there was plenty of time to enjoy the warm summer scenery – gentle hills and grassy plains heading down to the Black Sea. These days, it's impossible to feel the hot breeze rushing in from an open train window, at least in the UK. I think it's partly down to health and safety concerns (people might throw themselves/others/other objects out – the world's gone mad) and partly down to ensuring that air conditioning (when working) operates to maximum effect. But it felt both exhilarating and relaxing to me, as I sprawled across the seats that summer afternoon. It's also very loud of course, but still quite hypnotically restful, despite that.

By the time we arrived in Varna, there wasn't a lot of time to explore much of the city. As we made our way to the hotel, I was struck by the large numbers of tourists milling about. Varna has certainly made a good job of attracting them. I'd read it had become a popular seaside resort over the years but hadn't realised to what extent. Walking through the crowds, it felt very much like a Black

Sea Benidorm – burger bars, beach balls and bikinis. That's absolutely fine of course, but I have to admit to being a bit disappointed, having hoped to sense a brooding Gothic backdrop against which I could imagine Dracula's coffin being stowed aboard the Demeter. Of course, I know it never actually happened, but it would have been wonderful to have the feeling confirmed that it *could* have once been possible – in the same way, I suppose, that many thousands of people go to Verona every year to look at a balcony that a fictional Juliet didn't actually stand on wishing that a fictional Romeo had a different surname. And the same in London with Baker Street and Sherlock Holmes, no doubt. On a sunny summer evening amidst the beach vibe, however, it all just made me feel like a bit of a naive and overgrown schoolboy, holding onto ridiculous childhood notions – not even a Kiss-me-Quick Count to be seen. But a couple of beers and a burger later, it seemed like a very good place to be enjoying the evening sunshine, even if I didn't have to worry about what might happen after darkness fell.

R2 – Riga to Sigulda – on a Latvian regional train

Route: Riga – Zemitani – Jugla – Garkalne – Krievupe – Vangazi – Eglupe – Sigulda

Margaret and I were having a short break in the beautiful city of Riga. I hadn't expected to take to it as much as I did, and it had clearly thrived in the years since reclaiming its independence from the USSR. The old town centre with its imposing church spires was a revelation, full of colourful buildings that strongly reflected its important past as a member of the Hanseatic League. I loved the Town Hall Square, dominated by the very striking House of the Blackheads which was far more attractive than its name suggests. It's apparently named after the Brotherhood of the Blackheads (a medieval guild of merchants, but a perfect name for a teenage gang I sometimes see down the precinct).

After a couple of days, we thought it'd be nice to take the train out of the city and see a bit more of the surrounding countryside. Though we'd never previously heard of the town of Sigulda, a bit of research on Google suggested it would be an interesting destination for a trip out – and only about an hour away with regular trains there and back round the clock. We made our way to the station and were soon on a train heading to Lugazi, a town just short of the Estonian border. Talking of Estonia – it's something of an oddity that train services *within* each of the three Baltic States (Estonia, Latvia and Lithuania) have generally been fairly decent, but rail connections *between* them have ranged from dismal to appalling. This may be partly due to years of Soviet occupation, which prioritised a divide and conquer rail policy, favouring direct routes from the three capitals to Moscow rather than between each of the three neighbours.

Consequently, north-south (and vice versa) rail travel has

until recently been quite a challenge, characterised by lengthy travel times, circuitous routes, multiple changes and infrequent connections; a situation which has seen most inter-Baltic travellers take the bus or plane. Things have very recently jumped quite a few steps forward, however. You can now travel from Tallinn to Riga with a simple cross-platform change at the border. Unfortunately, however, this is on local trains which stop quite a lot and make it a ten hour journey. Since December 2023, there's been a direct daily train from Riga to Vilnius and back which takes four hours to cover the 350 km. There's also a new direct Vilnius to Warsaw train (nine hours). But the very big news is something called Rail Baltica – a huge international project aiming to streamline and modernise the entire rail corridor down from Helsinki via Tallinn, Riga, Kaunas, Vilnius and Warsaw. There's even talk of an undersea tunnel between Helsinki and Tallinn, but time will tell. 2030 is currently hailed as target completion date but, again, time will tell. When it is finished, it will certainly be a huge improvement on the current situation.

But back to the Riga – Sigulda train. It was one of those lovely blue-sky summer days, plenty warm enough without frying your face off. A pleasant breeze came in through the open windows and views of Riga (the biggest city in the Baltic countries) soon gave way to hills and rolling fields. I honestly don't think we emphasise the therapeutic nature of train travel enough. Just sitting there, relaxing and watching the fields go by felt incredibly soul-nourishing that afternoon – simple, easy and inexpensive (I think the hour's journey cost less than the equivalent of three Euros). Maybe it doesn't work for everybody and I certainly see how it wouldn't if you were stuck in the aisle for fifty minutes on a busy commuter train with someone's armpit in your face. But when the conditions are just right, I'd be hard pressed to think of anything better for de-stressing and distracting a busy brain.

Sigulda is in Latvia's Gauja National Park, a beautiful area that follows the Gauja River, and known for its rocky outcrops, sandstone cliffs and forests. The presence of scouts and nuns on the train (I'm pretty sure they weren't all part of the same group, and am also assuming they weren't on a Latvian stag do), somehow just confirmed the sense we were heading somewhere 'that'll do you good'. After a quick and appropriately wholesome lunch on arrival, we headed off to explore a little, soon coming across the town's 'new' castle built in the 1800s and after a while reaching its restored medieval castle. Had we been staying longer, there were plenty of hiking trails we could have followed to see caves and other natural wonders. But we were perfectly happy just taking our time, having a gentle wander and getting some fresh country air before heading back to the station. This train trip out into the Latvian countryside has stayed with me as such a lovely, relaxing afternoon and, on the train back into Riga, I decided that I should do this sort of thing more often when back at home – just get on the train and take myself off somewhere nice for a few hours. Human nature being what it is and all that, however, I have to despair a bit at my repeated failure to act on intentions.

Train travel thoughts R

If you're heading somewhere on a romantic mission to recapture a close sense of history, try not to get your hopes up too high; as I once heard an American teenager say outside the Colosseum after seeing the film *Gladiator*, 'What the hell happened to this place, man?'

If you're on a city break, it's often a good idea to look into where you could get a train out to one afternoon to break the pace and see a bit more of the country.

S

S1 - Stockholm to Oslo – on the SJ morning express

Route: Stockholm – Katrineholm – Hallsberg – Degerfors – Kristinehamn – Karlstad – Arvika – Kongsvinger - Oslo

This was a journey I made in January 2016, after spending a few days working in Stockholm. I'd arrived there early one evening after two flights and a day of hanging around in airports, so I decided it'd be a good idea to walk to the hotel. It was just under a kilometre away and I was more than ready to stretch my legs. I thought I was suitably attired for the Scandinavian winter, so what was there to stop me? I soon realised that minus 20 degrees centigrade was a bit harsher than the miserable Midlands morning on which I'd left Birmingham. I started off well but when I realised my glasses had frozen to my eyebrows, I thought it might be time to give in to my inner-wimp (a frequent defeat) and jump in a taxi. It won't be a shock to many people that January in Sweden tends to be on the cold side; I knew that too, but just hadn't quite expected it to be THAT cold but, as always, we live and learn. It was lovely walking into the hotel and feeling the warmth engulf me.

After the shock of the cold, my next surprise was to be asked a question I've never previously been asked at check-in – would I like a room with or without a window? When I asked if it made a difference in the price, the next shock was to hear that it certainly did. On that basis, I decided to go window-free – as I said, it was January in Sweden, how much light would be coming in anyway? So, prepared for a room without a view, I opened the door, only to find that the cheerful souls who owned the hotel had painted the walls black... so I was basically in a black box with a bed. I counted my blessings that I don't generally suffer from depression, otherwise this could have been quite a challenging stay. I'm still not sure what the thinking behind this was – was it stark Scando-minimalism? Was the manager a Goth? Was it a reflection of a brooding Nordic mindset? Or had there just been a special offer on *Dulux Dismal Night* down the market?

Whatever the reason, I thoroughly enjoyed the few days I spent in Stockholm, and really took a shine to the city. The days were crisp and bright (for a few hours) and the city architecture looked tremendous in the snow, set off against beautiful blue winter skies. The iconic view of Stockholm City Hall was just amazing. Looking at it on Kungsholmen Island from across the frozen water, it was magically mesmerising, like an impressionist painting come to life. I also took a chance on a visit to the Abba Museum – an absolute must for a child of the 70s and lifelong fan.

As reluctant as I was to say goodbye to my black box (obviously Stockholm Syndrome), I was very much looking forward to the 400 km train ride to Oslo. My train left at around 10.00, so there was no early morning rush to the station. And what a station Stockholm Central is! Built in the late 19th Century, huge arches sweep high above the concourse, creating a strong sense of railway gravitas. My train pulled in on time (as I'd somehow expected). The biggest surprise about this journey was actually the cost. Admittedly, my ticket had been booked in advance, but it was only £20. How could a six-hour rail journey of over 400 km cost only £20 – and in Scandinavia at that, home of the £10 pint??! Sometimes it seems you really can get a bargain. I think I was all the more amazed at the time, because I had travelled from Birmingham to London (164 km) a couple of months previously for over £140. I'll just leave that there.

I had a second class reservation but had to double-check once seated – the space, comfort and entire feel of the seat and carriage said first class to me – hats off to Swedish Rail (SJ). Faultless WiFi, onboard service, incredibly clean – this was definitely a good start. And again, £20..... The train pulled out right on time, and was soon travelling westwards out of the city into the Swedish countryside. Had this been summer, I dare say the scenery would have been more varied, but snow-covered as it was, it was difficult to tell what was field, lake or meadow. That really didn't bother me though – it was magical, a real full-on winter wonderland of endless forests and pristine white vistas, punctuated by little towns and villas here and there. I think I spent the first hour or so just mesmerised by this, it was difficult to look away, quite unlike any rail journey I'd ever been on before. And after my time in the Black Box, these endless expanses of white really were a welcome bit of therapy.

And so it continued for several hours, until gradually, the weak afternoon sunshine slipped away. The train crossed the border into Norway sometime after 14.00. At Kongsvinger, plain clothes customs officials and border police quietly walked through the train checking passports. There was nothing remotely stern or authoritarian about them, unlike the guards in many other countries – this was more like your mate's dad casually asking for a shufti at your passport, just out of interest. A few seats further down from me, they paused for quite a while though, in lengthy discussions with someone. After a short time, they escorted the passenger (I'd say of Middle Eastern origins) quietly off the train – quietly but firmly. It's anybody's guess what the full story was, and I could only speculate. But yet again, I was reminded of the fact that we're not all lucky enough to be able to cross borders when we want to. A short time afterwards, the train continued its journey, the Norwegian scenery flying past in much the same vein as the Swedish, interspersed by red-wood log cabins with snow-topped roofs. Eventually, we moved into Oslo's suburbs, and I was quite surprised how quickly the landscape transformed into an urban night scene. I'd underestimated how big a city Oslo is and, pulling into the Central Station after 16.00, there was no doubting I was arriving in a capital city. The station was buzzing, bright and welcoming as I moved through the bustling crowds, making their way to other connections or out into the city.

There are currently around five direct trains a day between Oslo and Stockholm. Given improvements in speed and service, and with some trains taking as little as five hours, there's no longer a need for night trains, though these still run to destinations further north in Norway. It's amazing to think there were once direct trains from Oslo to as far afield as Paris (on the North Express) and to Moscow via Gothenburg, Malmö and Berlin. The Skandia Express and the Alfred Nobel, both to Hamburg, survived until the early 1990s, but trains to Sweden are currently the only international connections from this charming city.

Visiting Oslo for the first time in a snowy January felt very special and, I suspect, made it more interesting than if I'd visited in the summer. It did make getting around on foot a bit harder, but I had the right footwear for it and a thick coat. The iconic red brick city hall (that wouldn't have looked out of place in Wolverhampton) definitely looked better for a covering of snow, and the view from outside up to the Akershus Fortress and across to the harbour was definitely more eye-catching – a stunning winterscape. The Royal Palace had the look of a real fairy-tale castle, perched as it was at the high end of a snowy path, and the Opera House was just magnificent – sophisticated and stately - and the views all around it overlooking the frozen Oslo fjord seemed a perfect accompaniment to this austere ice maiden of a building. I really enjoyed my time in the city – its charms may be gentle, but it's a friendly, easy-going place, even if your wallet might need full CPR by the time you leave.

S2 - Saint Petersburg to Velikiy Novgorod – on a Russian regional train

Route: Saint Petersburg – Rogavka – Veliky Novgorod

This was another journey Margaret and I did back in Russia in the early 90s. We'd arrived in Saint Petersburg on the White Nights train from Vologda – an overnight journey that took around twelve hours to cover the roughly 550 km between the two cities, so not exactly a high-speed express. I remember this journey quite affectionately. We were travelling with our younger Russian friend and guide, Dimitri, and had booked couchettes in a compartment for four people. The fourth place turned out to have been booked by an elderly Russian teacher who was travelling to visit relatives in Saint Petersburg. He spoke fluent English and was delightful company. He couldn't help but hear we were English and soon joined in the conversation. As so often happens, life details and stories were exchanged all round, and the journey turned into a lovely evening. Our travelling companion, whose name now escapes me (I'll call him Nikolai), insisted on sharing his food and vodka, and we of course reciprocated with what we had.

It's a really strange thing when you think about it. If I was on the train from Wolverhampton to Coventry and someone sitting opposite tried to share their vodka and chicken drumsticks with me, I'm fairly sure I'd get up and move to another carriage. But in the cocooned intimacy of a foreign railway compartment and a twelve hour journey, it seemed a totally natural and convivial exchange. Which is exactly what it was. So we chatted away and laughed, no doubt becoming slightly inebriated as the vodka bottle gradually emptied and, by late evening, we were bedding down in our respective bunks and snoozing into the small hours.

We arrived in Saint Petersburg at around 8.00 the next morning, feeling slightly the worse for wear, as is so often the case. Dimitri had organised for us to stay in an apartment which belonged to some family friends. They were apparently 'away' and had said very generously we were welcome to stay at their home (we suspected they'd just moved in with friends or family for a couple of days). The apartment wasn't too far from the station, Dimitri said... we'd become a little wary of Dimitri's distance calculations, as he was clearly operating on a very different system. It turned out to be about a three mile walk ('just another hundred metres') but it was good exercise, and of course incredibly kind of him to escort us. Once we reached the flat (in a tall Russian tenement block), Dimitri collected the key from a neighbour and in we went. It felt very strange staying in a total stranger's home when they're not there (it may have felt even stranger had they been, of course).

But the strangest thing about the place was the smell – an overpowering stench of decomposing bodies (animal, we hoped). When we lived in Holland, we occasionally had mice and rats find their way in underneath the house and then get trapped under the floorboards. There was no way to get at them without emptying out all the furniture and taking up all the floorboards, at considerable cost and effort... so we learned all you could do was grit your teeth and live through the initial decomposition phase when the smell was at its worst and, after about 4 weeks, the smell miraculously disappeared. I appreciate this isn't a very pleasant way to carry on, but sometimes you just have to crack on and wait for things to get better (please contact me for more expert counselling advice). From the smell in the Saint Petersburg apartment, I'd say several small rodents had recently pegged it and, unfortunately, we'd just have to put up with it – that was the price of free board and lodgings.

That said, we didn't spend a huge amount of time indoors as it was our first time in the city and there was a lot to see. And what an impressive city it is. In the early 90s, it wasn't receiving anything like the tourist numbers that flocked there in later years, and no doubt the current situation in Russia has again reduced visitor in-flows. But being able to view such a remarkable city without jostling with hordes of others felt incredibly special – standing on the palace square, looking at the huge expanse towards the Winter Palace and the Hermitage without a single other person in sight was just amazing, if not slightly eerie. The various rivers and canals that fill the city only added to this ethereal quality. Compared to the manic hustle and bustle of Moscow, the entire city felt so much calmer and exuded a sedate and peaceful elegance. We thought it was interesting that Dimitri preferred Moscow; he said Saint Petersburg was 'too prettified' and not truly Russian. Since Peter the Great had brought in engineers, architects, scientists, etc. from many countries across Europe to build the city, I suppose he had a point in a way.

The Grand Hotel Europe in the city centre really was a very pretty affair. We even managed to persuade Dimitri to have lunch with us there on one of the days (the alternative would have been to trudge back to the flat and see what, if anything, was available in the designated area shop). This must have been one of the few hotels at the time plushed up to posh Western European standards. Years later, we were amazed to see a documentary on Rasputin which showed him dancing in the ballroom there – the very room where we'd had lunch. As far as I'm aware, this is my only connection with Rasputin (my

Boney M record collection aside – and talking of Boney M – Bobby Farrell, the group's flamboyant frontman, died after a concert in the city in 2010... I'll say no more).

So, dying rodent smell apart (and an additional wildlife challenge I should mention – our two nights were plagued by the most persistent ear-bombing mosquitoes I've ever come across; Peter the Great had drained a swamp to build his city but it seemed nobody had told the mosquitoes), we really enjoyed our few days in Saint Petersburg. Our next journey was to be a relatively short one of about four hours (170 km) on a regional train to the historic city of Veliky Novgorod, reputedly the oldest city in Russia and apparently often referred to as the nation's birthplace. We headed back to Saint Petersburg's imposing Moscow Station and had no trouble finding seats. It was a pleasant enough journey but, once again, the scenery in much of Russia, especially the northern part, is nothing to write home about, unless you really love flat green plains punctuated by forests of silver birch trees.

We travelled in an open carriage, such as you'd commonly see in any commuter train anywhere in the world. People quietly munched on sandwiches, sat reading their books and newspapers, or chatted quietly with their travelling companions. I thought back to our recent overnight journey to Saint Petersburg and reflected again on the pleasant evening we'd spent chatting. I suppose there's something about undertaking a relatively short train journey that actively inhibits social contact and conversation. When you know it's just a few hours, we seem to adopt a mindset that tells us it's not worth investing the time and energy in establishing social bonds with strangers – or maybe I'm totally wrong, or just speaking for myself. Either way, it was a very peaceful journey, as the train trundled along, and it seemed no time at all before we arrived in Veliky Novgorod.

Our Russian friend in England was originally from Novgorod and had arranged for us to stay with her mother, Olga, who still lived there. She met us at the station and took us over to her apartment. I must say that all the Russians we met were incredibly hospitable and welcoming, and once again, it's such a terrible shame that the current situation in Russia has ended up demonising and isolating ordinary people in much the same way that they had been during the days of the Cold War. I have to admit to not knowing anything about Novgorod before we went there. The Veliky in the name (great) is used to distinguish it from Nizhny (lower) Novgorod on the Volga. We soon realised it's a remarkable small city, steeped in history (it was apparently here in 862 that the establishment of the Russian state was first declared). Small wonder that UNESCO added it to the list of world heritage sites. We were told it was one of the most important Eastern European cities in the Middle Ages, and one of the few Russian principalities to be saved from Mongolian invaders. Like many Russian cities, it has its own Kremlin, and very impressive it is too. Beautifully situated on the banks of the Volkhov River, it's a really picturesque place with plenty to see – ancient monasteries and churches, a monument to Rachmaninoff (who was born here), a wooden village museum, – suffice it say, well worth a visit. And like many people today, I wonder how long it'll be before the conflict in Ukraine is settled and Russia can once again be welcomed back into the international community.

Train travel thoughts S

Booking tickets in advance really can get you an absolute bargain - sometimes.

Now and again, it's a good thing to accept vodka and drumsticks from a stranger (discretion is always advised, however).

T

T1 - Tunis to Sousse on a Tunisian intercity

Route: Tunis – B. Bou Rekba – Kalaa Seghira - Sousse

The holiday David and I spent in Tunisia in the summer of 2010 couldn't have been a bigger contrast with the frozen Scandinavian winter I described above in S1. Stiflingly hot is an understatement. But despite the baking temperatures, we still wanted to explore as much as we could without killing ourselves in the heat. We'd taken the train north to Tunis and had had a really enjoyable time seeing the sights, of which there are plenty. I loved the combination of Mediterranean style and North African mystery – chic boulevards and meandering souks. I'd always fancied doing the entire journey by rail and sea from the UK, something still on the bucket list. (There was a time in the 1980s when Tunisia briefly considered joining Interrail, like its North African near-neighbour, Morocco, though it never actually came to fruition). These days it'd be easier and faster than ever before, of course – down to London for the Eurostar to Paris, then on to Marseille (or Genoa) for the ferry across the Med to Tunis, and all that in less than forty-eight hours.

As well as sightseeing in the capital, we decided to visit a hammam – a type of Turkish bath quite common throughout the Islamic world. We'd asked some locals for advice and the one we visited came highly recommended. We changed to shorts on entry and relaxed in the various sauna and steam rooms before we got to the massage stage. My initial impression of the masseur was slightly disconcerting – he was certainly getting on a bit and didn't look as if he'd be up for administering a vigorous pummelling. How wrong could I be though?! The other thing that threw me slightly was that he appeared blind in one eye. The only reason this slightly disturbed me was because it gave him a striking resemblance to the milky-eyed blind Arab in one of the opening scenes of the film *The Exorcist*, which features an extended introductory sequence in northern Iraq. I'd read that the director, William Friedkin, deliberately chose to dwell on this shot of the Arab's face as a kind of visual pre-cursor for what was about to follow. As the film progresses and the demon takes control, the face of possessed victim Linda Blair begins to echo said Arab's milky eye.

I couldn't stop all this going through my mind for a while, which is the last thing you need when you're just trying to relax and lull yourself into a state of calm oblivion. Eventually, the massage started to do the trick, however, and I felt the tension drifting away. The peace was disturbed yet again though when the old chap whispered into my ear, asking if he could... well, turn his attention to my own old chap and release further tension, shall we say. In case you're wondering, I politely declined this generously intimate and very unexpected offer. He didn't appear to take the refusal personally and carried on removing my epidermis with an industrial scrubbing brush.

After all this relaxation, awkwardness and steam, it was time for a steady stroll back to the station in the late afternoon heat. Although we'd bought our ticket that morning, we'd been told we had to validate it by getting it stamped in some office or other before we boarded the train. I knew this pre-travel validation practice was quite common in many countries but it usually involved just popping it into a ticket machine on the platform. After asking a few people, we eventually found the relevant place and waited in the queue for the required stamp. Then it was back to the platform to board the train to Sousse. The prices – by UK standards in 2010 – were amazingly cheap, so we'd decided to treat ourselves and travel first class and, I have to say, it really did feel like a treat. The carriage we sat in might have seen slightly better days, but it also had class. Smart wooden interiors, cotton headrests, air conditioning, comfortable and roomy seats – it reminded me of sophisticated train journeys I'd seen in old films. Glancing around, well-dressed business people sat reading French and Arabic newspapers, sipping drinks delivered by the passing waiter – very nice indeed.

We chatted away quietly but clearly not quietly enough not to be overheard. After a while, a woman from a row or two behind came forward and spoke to us – she was a fellow Brit, in fact a fellow Midlander, and she decided to come and join us for a chat. I say chat - it was more of a mass-offloading on her part, after the usual introductory-type questions. We didn't mind, however, as Sandra was quite a character and, by the sound of things, had been having a difficult time. We heard the full saga of how she'd been regularly travelling over to Tunisia to visit her much younger boyfriend. Few details were spared from what turned out to be a long and upsetting tale of financial woe, romantic abandonment and thwarted hopes. The outcome of it all was that she was on her way back to Monastir airport and Birmingham-bound, the planned marriage now well and truly off the cards. The two or so hour journey to Sousse seemed to fly by, and I was yet again reminded of how train journeys sometimes lead us into such fleeting intimacies with people we've never met before and are unlikely to ever again.

Arriving at the train station in Sousse, we said our good-byes to Sandra and bustled our way out into the busy city – Tunisia's third largest, in fact, and a truly impressive city it is too, with its UNESCO-listed medina and that same mix of dynamic exoticism and Mediterranean charm as Tunis. It's so sad and beyond horrendous that this is where the shocking ISIL terror attacks took place in 2015, killing thirty-eight holiday-makers in a mass shooting. Tourism suffered hugely - and understandably - in the wake of this tragedy, compounding the difficulties faced by so many ordinary Tunisians who rely on the tourist business for their livelihoods. I fully intend to go back to this fascinating country at some point, and hope to be able to tick the rail and ferry route off my bucket list.

T2 – Trieste to Ljubljana – on the Drava Express

Route: Trieste – Villa Opicina – Sezana – Divaca – Pivka – Postojna – Ljubljana

Trieste seems to be one of those places people are either not especially keen on or they fall in love with. I'm just basing this on regularly reading what people post on Facebook – lots of people saying they wouldn't rush back, others saying they could move there. It's odd how divisive it seems to be. As far as I'm concerned, I love it. And I'm not entirely sure why I do. I'm not alone in thinking this either. The travel writer Jan Morris devoted an entire book to her love affair with the city – *Trieste and the Meaning of Nowhere*. Associating the city with a sense of 'nowehereness' might seem a bit odd, especially from someone who really likes the place, but I think its 'out-on-a-limbness' is part of its melancholic appeal. It's tucked away down a strip of land at Italy's north-eastern end, a long way from the rest of the country; very close to and influenced by the former Yugoslav states but apart from them; and perched quietly on its own at the top of the Adriatic. Morris says:

> It is a middle-sized, essentially middle-aged Italian seaport, ethnically ambivalent, historically

confused, only intermittently prosperous...and so lacking the customary characteristics of Italy that in 1999 some 70% of Italians, a poll claimed, did not know it was in Italy at all.

Maybe it's something about having been the sort of person never to get picked for anything in PE at school that makes me both relate to and root for it (it hasn't got Venice's beauty, Florence's elegance, Rome's imposing might). I don't know, I could really be falling into the rambling zone now, so should possibly leave it – suffice it to say, I like it very much and have really enjoyed the few times I've been there over the years.

Despite its relative remoteness, the city was once, at least in transport terms, very far from 'nowhere.' In fact it used to be directly connected to major cities right across Europe even as far as Athens and Istanbul. This was partly due to its location on the main line from Rome and Venice to the Balkans and beyond. Sadly, many of these direct connections have long since fallen away. The following table shows the direct rail destinations that were still available from Trieste in the 1980s and in some cases into the 1990s:

Austria	Salzburg (Italy Austria Express), Vienna (Gondoliere Express)
Croatia	Zagreb, Vinkovci (Simplon Express, Drava Express,

	Kras)
France	Calais, Paris (Simplon Express), Toulouse
Germany	Munich (Italy Austria Express through coach), Hamburg and Puttgarden (Alpen Express through coach), Dusseldorf, Berlin
Hungary	Budapest (Venezia Express, Drava Express)
Italy	Milan, Venice, Florence, Rome, Lecce, etc.
Romania	Timisoara, Bucharest, Cluj Napoca (Venezia Express)
Russia	Moscow
Serbia	Belgrade (Venezia Express, Nikola Tesla)
Slovenia	Ljubljana (Drava Express, Venezia Express, Kras)
Switzerland	Zürich (Canaletto), Geneva (Simplon Express)
Ukraine	Kiev

This particular visit was on an Interrail trip in the late

1990s. It had been great revisiting the sights – the iconic view of the Chiesa di Sant Antonio at the end of the Grand Canal, the huge Piazza dell Unita d'Italia (the biggest seafront square in Europe), and even the Roman amphitheatre; not exactly the Colosseum but still - it's a Roman amphitheatre. I've always loved the wonderful seafront promenade, especially the evocative statues of the chatting seamstresses. There's something about them sitting there quietly on the edge of the Adriatic that wonderfully encapsulates the city's sense of dignified isolation for me. After a couple of days, I was now heading off to Ljubljana, the capital of Slovenia. At this point in time, the city still enjoyed regular rail connections with its near neighbour. Though this had once been a major international rail corridor, as the table above shows (and the same route used by the old Simplon Orient Express), direct services from Trieste to Slovenia and beyond were cancelled in the early 2000s but restored and extended more recently. Shortly after midday, it was sadly time to say 'Adieu Trieste/Bonjour Tristesse' as I boarded the Drava Express.

Named after the Drava River in Slovenia (and several other countries), its ultimate destination would be Budapest via Ljubljana. It had left Venice around two hours earlier that morning; for several years, it ran to and from Venice in the summer months only, and from Trieste for the rest of the time. The train had originally been introduced as a daytime counterpart to the

Venezia/Venice Express which covered the same route by night. In its day, the Venezia Express carried an impressive collection of through coaches to various destinations in Eastern Europe and the Balkans – some travelling east after Budapest to destinations in Romania, Ukraine and Russia (see the above table), while other sleepers headed down through the former Yugoslavia. Up until the 1970s, there were even carriages bound for Greece and Turkey.

It was pleasantly quiet for a summer Sunday, so I had no problem finding a seat or, indeed, a compartment all to myself. The train hugged the Adriatic coast for quite a while before looping round and heading towards the Slovenian border. En route, it passed through the now disused Prosecco station (the town which gave its name to what you'd expect). Villa Opicina is the Italian border station, and in no time at all we stopped again in Sezana where the Slovenian border guards got off. The journey up to Ljubljana from this point was delightful – views all around of lush green hills and forests, set off beautifully by the summer sunshine. Not too long before the capital, on the approach to Borovnica, the train passed through a spectacular valley, with amazing views from the left-hand side of the train. And three hours or so after leaving Trieste, we pulled into Ljubljana's station. My first port of call was a depot stop, thinking it might be quieter than on a week day and bored railwaymen might be more inclined to humour my enquiries about train signs; my hunch paid off remarkably well, and I headed off to the hotel I'd booked, far more weighed down than when I'd stepped off the train.

Ljubljana itself is a charmingly small capital city with a great atmosphere and signs of its Austro-Hungarian past everywhere in its architecture. It's a fantastic place to saunter around, stopping for a drink and a spot of people-watching on one of its many little squares. I was intrigued to see dragon symbols all over the city, and most obviously the statues adorning Dragon Bridge. I was delighted to discover that (according to legend) on their way back from collecting the Golden Fleece, Jason and his Argonauts stopped off near Ljubljana to slay a dragon (as you do), since which time the beast has come to symbolise the city's might and courage. Like most legends, this is no doubt total bunkum, but learning of this story was another lovely loop-making moment in life; the 1963 film *Jason and the Argonauts* had been one of my childhood obsessions for years, after seeing it on TV in my primary school years. Like the dragons though, the Drava Express itself is also no more. It survived a while longer before being upgraded and slightly rerouted (to exclude Trieste but include Zagreb) as the fairly short-lived EC Goldoni service. There is currently no direct service between Venice/Trieste and Budapest, but at least the Trieste to Ljubljana section has been reinstated, making Trieste a little less 'nowhere' than it had been.

Train travel thoughts T

Always check if you have to validate your ticket somehow pre-departure; even tickets bought online sometimes require pre-travel validation.

If you know you're going to be travelling along a very scenic route, it's worth doing a bit of research to check which side of the train will offer you the best views.

U

U – Utrecht to the Hook of Holland – on the Scandinavia Holland Express

Route: Utrecht – Schiedam-Rotterdam West – Hook of Holland

Anyone familiar with Dutch geography will look at this and realise very quickly it isn't one of the world's longest railway journeys. And what's more, this particular stretch is unlikely to ever feature in anyone's list of greatest ever rail trips – apart from mine, and that for a few reasons... as I'll explain. The first reason is that when I was a language student, I spent my year abroad at the University of Utrecht and so this is a journey I ended up making lots of times that year in particular, and many more times over the years that followed; so, in short, it's a trip that's ended up being very close to my heart. Secondly, it's a journey that involves the Hook of Holland – not exactly Paris or Rome, but a special place that made a big impression on me in my formative years. And thirdly – this short stretch of around an hour may initially seem fairly insignificant but it's part of a longer route that holds an important place in international railway history. And one final reason, if I'm being totally honest - the only other contender for 'U' was a twenty minute rail journey from Uttoxeter to Stoke-on-Trent that anybody would be hard pressed to say much about (no disrespect to either of these towns!).

So, as I was saying, back in my student days this was a regular trip. I was living in a rented room just a short distance from Utrecht Central Station, so hauling my stuff backwards and forwards between home and station became a regular occurrence. Utrecht itself is a really lovely small city. It is, of course, eclipsed by its bigger neighbour, Amsterdam, just a half hour's train ride away, so it gets nothing near the immense numbers of tourists who visit the capital. In a way that's a shame, as it's a charming city with plenty to see. The historic centre is a fantastic place to mooch about, with lots of little streets and alleyways leading off the 'Oude Gracht' (old canal) that runs right through the city and easily rivals anywhere in Amsterdam for atmosphere and picturesque views. The medieval centre is dominated by the cathedral, de Dom, which has the tallest belfry in the Netherlands. The views from the top are really quite amazing. Because it's spared the massive hordes of tourists that increasingly plague Amsterdam (recently, the city council there has in fact been working on campaigns to actively deter visitors), Utrecht often manages to give you a more authentic sense of Holland; you can easily walk around and take in the views without sharing them with bus loads of Chinese tourists and British stag parties.

In the time I spent there in the 1980s, it was wonderful having a coffee and a cheap brandy (how sophisticated was I?) in one of the many brown cafes, watching the world go by. Brown café is the term used by the Dutch to describe a kind of traditional, dimly lit café. There always seemed to be some discussion as to why they were called brown – it was partly down to the dark wooden interiors and carpets, but equally down to the heavy clouds of tobacco smoke that added to the browning effect and atmosphere. At busy times, you couldn't always see who was sitting opposite you. Sometimes, that was a good thing. These days the cigarettes have, of course, disappeared and there seems to be a question about their future – do people still want to drink in old-fashioned, cosy cafes? I certainly hope they manage to survive and resist the trend towards the homogenised trendy and the flash; time will tell.

But back to the train - the hour's journey from Utrecht to the Hook was always a straightforward trip. The industrially-ironed Dutch landscape soon whizzed past, and before all too long the train entered the sprawling urban dock-scape of Rotterdam and environs. Once arrived in the Hook, it was a just short hop through customs and onto the boat for the night (or sometimes day) crossing to Harwich. Having made the long trek down from Stockholm, Copenhagen and Hamburg, the Scandinavia Holland Express arrived in Utrecht at around 21.18, reaching the Hook an hour later. At that time in the 1980s, another added bonus of travelling this route was the decent number of direct trains from Harwich Parkeston Quay station (or Harwich International, as it later became known) heading all over the UK. There were frequent boat trains to London, as well as the Midlands, the North West and Scotland. For a time, some of these trains bore names that reflected their international connections, e.g. the Rhinelander (to and from Manchester), the European (Glasgow and Edinburgh), the Admiraal de Ruijter and Benjamin Britten (London – in fact these trains were the only UK ones ever to carry the EuroCity designation for a short time in 1986/7. The distinction was short-lived as the trains failed to meet the internationally agreed quality standards expected – who'd have thought?). In addition, there were the Vincent van Gogh (Liverpool) and the Britannia and the Loreley (both Manchester and Blackpool). In the case of the these last two trains, it meant that there were two services from the North West of England via the Hook to Switzerland and Italy that went under the same name for the entire route from Manchester to Rome – something of a railway novelty. In my view, it's a real shame we don't name trains any more in Britain – for me, getting on 'The Loreley' in Birmingham New Street always gave me a mini-thrill (ok, still acknowledging my need to get out more).

The table below shows a list of some of the main named boat train services of the past. Those with an asterisk operated between 1900 (and sometimes earlier) and the 1950s; the other trains ran chiefly in the 1980s and early 1990s. Some of these trains ran on slightly amended routes in certain years (e.g. from Derby rather than

Manchester in some timetable periods, etc).

Boat train name	From	To (and vice versa)
Admiraal de Ruyter (EC)	London Liverpool Street	Harwich
Antwerp Continental*	London Liverpool Street	Harwich
Benjamin Britten (EC)	London Liverpool Street	Harwich
The Britannia	Manchester	Harwich
Brussels Boat Train*	London Victoria	Dover
The Continental*	Liverpool	Folkestone
The Day Continental*	London Liverpool Street	Harwich
The Dover Pullman Express*	London Victoria	Dover
Esbjerg Continental Express*	London Liverpool Street	Harwich
The European	Edinburgh/Glasgow	Harwich

The Essex Continental*	London Liverpool Street	Harwich
The Flushing Continental*	London Liverpool Street	Harwich
The Golden Arrow*	London Victoria	Dover
The Hook & Antwerp Continental*	London Liverpool Street	Harwich
The Loreley	Blackpool/Birmingham	Harwich
The Norseman*	London Kings Cross	Newcastle
The North West Dane	Blackpool	Harwich
The Parisienne	London Waterloo	Portsmouth
The Rhinelander	Manchester	Harwich
The Scandinavian*	London Liverpool Street	Harwich
The Vincent Van Gogh	Liverpool	Harwich
The Zeebrugge Continental*	London Liverpool Street	Harwich

One other reason for my Utrecht-Hook (and vice versa) soft spot is that doing this journey ended up becoming deeply imbued with a sense of excitement – heading to the Hook meant going home, catching up with friends and family, and having a break; and in the reverse direction, it meant leaving the confines of home behind me, heading back to new friends, and enjoying the fun of being a student abroad. I also remember the times I did this journey with a whole range of travelling companions – mates, the occasional lover and my wife. So for me, this is one journey that feels incredibly close and personal, connected as it is to the people and experiences that ended up making their marks on my life.

The personal significance the Hook has for me actually developed a few years before my student days. Still at school in 1981, I took part in a German exchange scheme. We travelled by coach to Harwich for the overnight crossing and arrived in the Hook the following morning. As we walked from the boat and through to the station, I can still remember the sense of magical wonderment I felt when I looked up at the departures board. Coming from a small Midlands town where getting even to Birmingham often seemed a trial, let alone anywhere else in the country, there was something almost intoxicating about this accessibly exotic mix of trains waiting on the platforms, soon to head off to almost every corner of Europe. The teachers rounded us up and ushered us on to the Holland Scandinavia Express, due to leave at 7.10 that morning.

To my teenage self, this seemed like something from a film. Like lots of my working class contemporaries, kids growing up in the 1970s and 1980s had not generally been spoiled in the way that a lot of today's children are. Many of my friends' children think nothing of flying half way round the globe for a week because they've been doing it regularly since before they could talk. But to the 15-year-old me, whose travel experience had been the bus to Wolverhampton and occasional holidays in Blackpool and Cornwall, this trip to Germany felt like being in a TV glamour documentary (though I'm sure that would have been the last thing anyone looking at us would have thought). I glanced at the destination sign as we got on the train, scanning all the stops between the Hook and Copenhagen, and felt that life was finally taking off... We travelled through Holland and over the border into the German town of Rheine, where we had to change for our connection to Leer in north Germany (see G2). But by that time, the seed of my lifelong fascination with train travel was well and truly planted.

The number and range of destinations from the Hook of Holland in those days was genuinely impressive, as the table below shows. In earlier years, there had even been direct connections from the Hook to Prague, Vienna and Athens, but by 1981, the list was still considerable.

Some of the international trains from the Hook of

Holland (1970s and 80s):

Train Name	Key Destinations
Austria Express	Cologne, Bonn, Stuttgart, Munich, Salzburg, Klagenfurt, Graz
Boat train Amsterdam	The Hague, Amsterdam
Britannia Express	Cologne, Bonn, Heidelberg, Stuttgart, Munich, Innsbruck, Bolzano, Merano (Italian Dolomites)
Colonia Express	Cologne
East West Express	Berlin, Warsaw, Minsk, Moscow
Holland Scandinavia Express	Osnabrück, Bremen, Hamburg, Copenhagen, Stockholm
Hook Warsaw Express	Hanover, Berlin, Warsaw
Loreley (Express)	Cologne, Basle, Chur, Chiasso; Milan, Florence, Bologna, Rome
North Express/North West Express	Hamburg, Copenhagen, Stockholm
Rheingold (TEE)	Cologne, Basle, Lucerne,

	Lausanne, Geneva, Milan
Rhine Express	Cologne, Dortmund, Stuttgart, Munich, Innsbruck
Vorarlberg Express	Munich, Innsbruck
(unnamed)	Bad Harzburg

Not all of the trains in the table travelled on the section between Utrecht and the Hook, though a good many did, perhaps most notably the legendary Trans Europe Express Rhinegold, on its way to and from the Hook and Geneva/Milan. The Holland Scandinavia Express and its nightly counterpart, the North West Express, had been regular visitors since the 1950s, as had the East West Express bound for Berlin, Warsaw, Minsk and Moscow. I often 'intercepted' this train at Utrecht station in the late 1980s on its way to the Hook. My friend Marek, who worked for Polish Railways, was a great supplier of the destination signs I collect. I returned the favour with batches of railway magazines. Back then, he suggested sending me regular supplies (suitably disguised in 'brown paper packages') with a colleague of his who worked as a sleeping car attendant on the train. So on mutually agreed evenings, I'd head to Utrecht station at the pre-arranged time, feeling like a spy on work placement. I'd wait for the train to pull in, quickly try and identify the Polish carriage and then seek out said colleague for 'package exchange' to take place.

At the time, this felt like quite a risky Cold War thrill, exchanging mysterious parcels on an international train, and I can certainly remember getting quizzical looks off passengers who happened to witness the exchange. There was one particularly memorable time when it was a very inebriated attendant (a last-minute substitute) who had no idea what I was talking about (inevitable at times in the days before email and mobiles) and decided to escort me quite aggressively off the train. Another time, I also remember it took me a bit longer than usual to track down the Polish guard... and I ended up stuck on the train to Rotterdam before I had the chance to get off and head back home. Happy days!

The beautiful Neo-Renaissance station at the Hook was built as long ago as 1893, when travellers first started arriving on ferries from Harwich and from even further afield on the Holland America Line steamships. Exactly one-hundred years later in 1993, the last ever international train left the station, bound for Moscow. Yet again, the competition from cheaper air fares and the imminent opening of the Channel Tunnel saw dwindling numbers of travellers. I have to admit to feeling quite sad that today not a single train (not even from Utrecht), let alone an international train, leaves from or visits the Hook. It's been demoted from being one of the principal gateways to the Continent to an end of the line stop on the

Rotterdam metro – the railway equivalent of going from Hollywood stardom to a bit part on *Crossroads*. But for me, it'll always be its early Brando years I remember.

Train travel thoughts U

It's a good idea to look into nearby places worth visiting when you're on a city break – most Amsterdams have an Utrecht nearby (e.g. Ghent for Brussels, Como for Milan, Lucerne for Zurich, etc).

If anyone suggests exchanging parcels on a train, you're probably better off using the post.

V

V1 – Vienna to Gdansk – on the Chopin night train

Route: Vienna – Hohenau – Breclav – Ostrava – Bohumin – Petrovice u Karvine – Zebrzydowice – Katowice – Sosnowiec – Warsaw – Ilawa – Malbork – Tczew - Gdansk

This was another journey on one of my 1990s Interrail trips. I'd spent a couple of days in Vienna, seeing the sights, drinking beer and relaxing. I really like Vienna, though I know quite a lot of people who didn't overly take to it. I'm not entirely sure what they expected but I love the grand palaces and the imposing imperial architecture that fills the city. I get that its charms are not exactly subtle, and I can see how you might eventually feel a bit oppressed by its solid, clunky chunkiness (not an architectural term). I think some also underestimate its size and scale – it's a huge city and it feels like it. For most of its history, Vienna was in fact the biggest city in the German-speaking world (until it got overtaken by Berlin at the start of the 20th Century). There can also be a chokingly stolid wealthy/class vibe that is sometimes a little off-putting – the opera jet-set, the flash and so beautifully-dressed business crowd, the Mozart and Klimt cognoscenti, the smug lady cliques doing cake and coffee... or maybe that's just me and my working-class roots feeling like an imposter. But for all that, I like it, and it's well worth heading out of the centre to the little

Heuriger wine taverns where you get a sense of a more relaxed and down-to-earth Vienna – especially after a few drinks.

As with all Interrail trips, the time comes to move on to the next leg, and for me this was a trip up to Gdansk via Warsaw. The Chopin night train was due to leave just before 22.00 that evening, so plenty of time to get to what was then Vienna Südbahnhof (one of the city's two main railway stations at the time, the other being the Westbahnhof; in 2009 a new central station was built to accommodate most national and international train services). I'd pre-booked a couchette berth and was hoping I might be lucky enough to have the compartment to myself. It turned out I wasn't, but walking up and down the carriage, it didn't appear to be particularly busy. I had a word with the attendant and asked if there was a chance of switching to one of the empty compartments – asking the question with a modest bank note in my hand worked wonders, and with a wink and a smile, mission accomplished – good night Vienna.

Another small win, and one which by and large is difficult to achieve in this day and age where night trains often run at full capacity. This was one of those uneventful evenings that somehow seemed quite perfect. I locked the compartment door, opened the train window wide and stood leaning out, beer in hand, suddenly overwhelmed by an almost 'grand tourist' sense of romance. Maybe it was just what Paul Theroux once described:

> The romance associated with the sleeping car derives from its extreme privacy, combining the best features of a cupboard with forward movement.

Whatever it was, it was a beautiful summer evening and, by this point, I think I'd been on Interrail for about three weeks. Suddenly that evening I remember thinking that it didn't feel like I was on holiday any more – it felt as if this was just my life now – this was what I did. Getting the train from place to place, visiting countries and people and then moving on to do more of the same. For the first couple of weeks, you're doing the exact same things of course, but with an awareness that you're operating outside the normal scheme of things. That night, for some reason, it all just suddenly felt as if this *was* my normal routine, and I'd totally relaxed into it. As the train pulled out of the station, the sprawling Viennese suburbs rattling by, I really had the feeling that this is how life should be all the time. It's odd but I find it difficult to describe how suddenly and completely overwhelmed I was by a sense of freedom and purpose. Nothing to worry or care too deeply about, no niggling questions about life and work – enjoying the journey and getting to the next destination were all that mattered.

In the 1990s, Vienna was (and has since again become) one of the best-connected railway hubs in Europe.

Trains departed from its two main stations to virtually every corner of the Continent, as they had for decades – to Amsterdam, Paris and Copenhagen; to Istanbul, Athens and Rome; Bucharest, Moscow and... well, just about everywhere. As is clear by now, this network of direct international night trains drastically reduced in the years that followed but it's heartening – and to me, feels totally fitting – that Vienna has begun to reclaim its position as European railway hub par excellence in more recent years.

I'm sure many people reading this will be au fait with the Nightjet story. For those less familiar, Nightjet is the brand name of Austrian Railways' (ÖBB) overnight train services. It was launched in 2016, at a point when just about all of Western Europe's railway services had decided to abandon running night trains. It was the usual story – the challenge of competing with ubiquitous and ridiculously cheap air fares; changing passenger habits and expectations; and a railway industry that by and large had been too slow to adapt and respond. Sensing an opportunity among all these challenges, ÖBB decided to launch a new generation of night trains. Initially, the number of services wasn't huge but gradually more and more routes have been added, putting Vienna, Salzburg and Innsbruck once again back at the centre of night train travel in Europe. It may have seemed quite a gamble at the time but it has certainly paid off, with most routes now fully booked up several months in advance. Some of this is down to post-pandemic preferences – some people preferring to avoid crowded airports and planes by opting for the individual and couples compartments available on many Nightjet routes. But the bigger reason no doubt relates to changing environmental attitudes and the growing phenomenon of 'flight shame' which mean that more people are now inclined to see trains as preferable to flying. So I well and truly take my hat off to ÖBB and, though I've not yet had a chance to travel on a Nightjet myself, I look forward to doing so in the near future.

The Chopin night train still runs today, though as an EN service with upgraded comfort and with a slightly longer route via Krakow. The rest of my journey was comfortable and quiet, outside of the inevitable knocks on the door from border guards as we passed into the Czech Republic (only an hour or so after leaving Vienna) and then again in the middle of the night on entering Poland. For all that, I arrived in Warsaw feeling reasonably refreshed at just after 8.00 the next morning, ten hours after leaving Vienna. I jumped on the next Polish intercity train for the final part of the journey, another 280 km that took about three hours, getting me into Gdansk before lunch. Like many people who were teenagers in the 1980s, Gdansk brought to mind images of the Lenin shipyard, the Solidarity struggles and political upheaval that never seemed off the TV news screens at the time. But there's far more to it than that – in fact, it's an enchanting city and not surprisingly one of Poland's most visited. Situated on the Baltic coast, this former Hanseatic town wouldn't look out of place in Holland, with its handsome guild houses and churches (the Dutch did in fact have much architectural and engineering involvement). In no time at all, I was sitting on a terrace with a burger and a beer, taking it all in for the first time, and marvelling how I'd gone from the Danube to the Baltic in what seemed like the blink of an eye.

V2 – Vienna to Bratislava – on a regional express

Route: Vienna – Marchegg – Devinska Nova Ves – Bratislava

This was another journey on a mid-1990s Interrail trip, and at one hour and 65 km, a very short and easy one between these two European capitals. Back then there were just a few trains a day, a very different situation from the almost half-hourly service of today. It's strange to think these two places once sat in two divided worlds on either side of the Iron Curtain and that they're now just local neighbours once again (as they were for most of their history). Talking of history, Bratislava has long been an important city at the heart of central Europe. Although it's now the capital of Slovakia, it was once the capital of neighbouring Hungary for over two-hundred years (up to 1784). The historical significance of a city is sometimes reflected in its having different names in different languages, and this is particularly true when it comes to Bratislava. It's known as Pozsony in Hungarian and historically as Pressburg in German and English. This apparently caused some confusion for travellers a few years ago when the city was first absorbed into the wider network of EuroCity trains; it was reported that German Rail (having done due dictionary diligence, fair play) announced the arrival of trains to the city in English using the now archaic name, Pressburg. This left lots of Bratislava-bound travellers hanging around on the platform as the train they wanted to board happily went off on its way... whoops! A mistake easily corrected of course once it was drawn to DB's attention by annoyed and delayed passengers.

Dwelling briefly on the city's name, some people might have wished Quentin Tarantino and Eli Roth *had* decided to opt for using Pressburg rather than Bratislava when they chose to set part of their 2005 horror film *Hostel* in the city. If you're unfamiliar with the film, it's a notorious horror movie that revolved around three American tourists getting abducted and sadistically murdered in the city – admittedly not the best PR for any town. Reaction across Slovakia was pretty severe, with many claiming the film did lasting damage to the country's image and tourist industry. The director Eli Roth was even invited to Bratislava to try and set the record straight and give the city some positive publicity. As mentioned, my visit there was in the mid 90s before all this kicked off but I'm pretty sure it wouldn't have put me off. Though I haven't actually been back since...

The late morning train I was travelling on from Vienna was fairly quiet and I was able to sit back and relax (untroubled by thoughts of gratuitous sexual torture) as we moved eastwards through the Viennese suburbs towards the Slovak border. I'm always fascinated by suburbs – there's something captivating about these often bland places on the edge and in between, close...but no cigar. At Marchegg, the last town in Austria, there was a brief and cursory passport check and, minutes later, we arrived in Devinska Nova Ves, where I noticed a large group of railway workers loading crates and boxes into containers on the opposite platform. The only reason this memory has stayed with me is because it made me think of Dracula (sorry, I'm at it again): in Bram Stoker's book, he describes the workers dealing with the Count's cargo of coffins as Slovaks (I wonder if this is what created a sinister association with Slovaks for Eli Roth?). I'm not sure why there would have been Slovak cargo workers in Transylvania, but then Dracula is a work of fiction and maybe I'm overly fixated.

Moving on, it was only a matter of minutes before we were trundling through Bratislava's suburbs. Back then, they still had a distinctive Eastern European look – a profusion of drab concrete buildings, litter and general dilapidation. (To be fair, I still get that same feeling today when approaching the outskirts of many Midlands towns. I'd imagine Bratislava's suburbs have probably moved on considerably by now.) Arriving at the city's main station,

Hlavna Stanica, I decided to try my luck down the depot and see if I might be able to negotiate a few additions to my sign collection. Communication in German and English didn't seem to be getting me anywhere, and I quickly realised I wasn't exactly playing to a receptive audience. After a few minutes of gruff shrugging and aggressive Slavic noises that sounded very much like 'f**k off', I thought I'd probably be best making tracks, and so set off to explore the city centre.

It was a good walk up to the castle (no Dracula reference this time), perched on top of a rocky hill with great views over the Danube and the rest of the city. It was one of those days where I seemed to walk miles and miles, stopping off here and there in the old town to admire the view or have a drink. I called in at a little street-side cafe and was handed a menu. A quick glance revealed that all items were in Slovak... and of course, why shouldn't they be? I asked if they had an English or German menu but received a curt shake of the head from the unsmiling waitress. Fair enough. This meant I could either be adventurous and just pick something randomly, or go with the safe bet of 'cheeseburger' – which is what I ordered. A short time later, the waitress came back with a cheese sandwich (still no smile). When I queried the lack of burger, she pointed gruffly at the cheese filling, saying 'Cheese'; then she pointed at the bread and said 'Burger'. I thought it wise to leave things be and crack on with my cheese sandwich – life goes on without a burger, for probably a few minutes longer, if truth be told.

After more walking and sightseeing, I realised it was probably a good idea to get back to Vienna, where I was staying for a couple of days, so asked for directions to the station. I'd clearly lost track of how far I'd walked, as people were suggesting it was about 4 km away, and by that point, there was no way I was doing that on foot. Once I'd been pointed to a nearby bus stop, I then faced the challenge of sorting a ticket. It seemed to be a day dogged by communication challenges – I just couldn't make myself understood, so I ended up braving the ticket machine at the stop. Easier said than done sometimes, of course. The short version is – it was unfathomable. I pressed, I guessed, I inserted coins, but nothing. Then the bus came – so I followed the other waiting passengers, jumped on in the middle and sat down.

It seemed an interminable ride, and knowing I was travelling without a valid ticket was making me incredibly – and ridiculously - tense. What if there was an on-the-spot inspection? What would happen? Thank God I hadn't seen *Hostel* at that point. After several more minutes of scanning each approaching stop for inspectors and feeling like Slovakia's most wanted fraudster, I could take it no more, so got off the bus and ended up walking the final kilometre to the station. By the time I got there, I'd missed the last direct train back to Vienna for quite a few hours. This meant I ended up heading back via Breclav in the Czech Republic – a slightly circuitous route but at least I could sit down and enjoy the ride and a rest.

As mentioned, current links between Vienna and Bratislava are fast and frequent, as they are to Prague and Budapest. In fact, the city is nicely positioned on the major rail route that links Hamburg with Budapest via Berlin, Dresden and Prague. Even in Iron Curtain days, this corridor was one of the most important routes between the northern and southern Communist states. Probably the most famous and important train from those days in this respect was the Pannonia Express, a train which travelled down from Berlin to Sofia via Prague, Bratislava, Budapest and Bucharest - a journey of two nights. Maybe this is how Dracula's Slovaks got down to Transylvania... again, I'm over-thinking.

Train travel thoughts V

Try and visit a Heuriger if you're in Vienna.

Don't expect to settle into Interrailing immediately – it usually takes some time to get comfortable.

Obvious I know, but check out city names in different languages – sometimes they look nothing like what you'd expect (Liège is Luik in Dutch, Milan is Mailand in German... and Munich is Monaco in Italian!)

Be sure to pace yourself on Interrail trips; it's easy to end up completely exhausted from so much walking and sightseeing.

A cheeseburger is not always a cheeseburger – ancient saying.

Always buy a bus ticket, unless you've got the nerves and self-defence abilities of Jason Statham.

W

W - Wolverhampton to Lyon – on the 'Houston Express' (and several other trains and a boat)

Route: Wolverhampton – London Euston/Victoria – Dover – Calais – Paris Nord – Paris Lyon – Dijon - Lyon

This is another journey that I don't think ever featured in anyone's Grand Tour, but it's one that I look back on with great affection. This was in 1984. Before starting my languages degree at university, I'd spent several months as a teaching assistant at a German school (see H1 – Heidelberg to Ostend). Once I'd finished in Germany, I managed to arrange a similar stint working at a French school in rural Auvergne, and now it was time to get there. Though I'd been to Germany quite a few times at that age (19), I'd only ever been to France once, and that was a week's camping trip to Dunkirk with a mate from school. Not exactly Club 18-30, but for two Midlands lads who'd never travelled much, it seemed quite an exotic adventure at the time. So the prospect of now travelling solo deep into unknown French territory did feel a little daunting, and I remember being quite nervous about it.

The journey began on a Sunday morning when my sister drove me and my mother (not exactly the butchest of send-offs) to nearby Wolverhampton railway station to pick up a London-bound intercity. For a time in the

1980s, there were a few direct trains from the North West and the Midlands that went straight to Dover, bypassing London by travelling through Kensington Olympia. Catching one of these would have been a godsend but the timings never seemed to work out for my connections somehow, so it was the usual trek to and through the capital. Seasoned travellers that we weren't, I'll always remember someone on the platform asking my mother if the train coming in was the one for London; "Yes," said my mother, "this is the Houston Express" (God bless her). I remember smiling to myself and it's one of those small but touching memories that comes to mind every time I've boarded a train to London Euston ever since.

Minutes later, I too was on board and Euston-bound, waving my mother and sister goodbye like a big softie, and feeling apprehensive about the journey ahead. We take it for granted these days that cases have wheels, but back then, it was far from the case (weak pun again intended). So lugging the luggage was always a challenge, especially when you couldn't get hold of a trolley, and that in itself was an additional teenage worry for me. Pulling into Euston, the unpleasant slog to Victoria Station ensued and, as always, it felt like a mini triumph when you got there. I still remember looking up at the departure boards there and seeing Continental destinations listed – yet again, it seemed so exotic, exciting and 'un-Midlands'. Before all too long, I was on the train to Dover, relieved that the London leg was done and dusted. And a couple of hours later, the usual foot passenger shuffle followed, as the train emptied and everyone headed for the ferry.

Foot passengers were always directed to leave their luggage in designated locker rooms once on the ferry. This was obviously sensible, as hundreds of people milling about dragging luggage wouldn't really have been in anyone's interest, but I always felt uneasy about doing this. What if somebody took my stuff? Who would I report it to? How would I get/afford new stuff? It seemed a bit unsettling and I was always much relieved to get it back when the ferry docked. Once in Calais, it was time for the repeat shuffle as everyone amassed at the exit and onto the walkway off the ferry and into the station at Calais Maritime – a station that sadly no longer even exists (it closed in the run-up to the opening of the Channel Tunnel in 1994).

The ferry services from Folkestone and Dover called in at Calais practically round the clock and, once off the boat, passengers would soon find themselves walking out into the Maritime Station where trains stood waiting to whisk them off across the Continent. (It's sad to think that, in recent years, most of the ferries no longer even take foot passengers – only those on coaches or in cars.) The 'Gare Maritime' had originally been built in 1849 but was replaced by a larger station in 1889. Damaged during the Second World War, it was eventually replaced by a fairly non-descript modern structure in 1956 – the one which most of us travelling by train from Calais will remember, though its fairly austere post-war bland concrete design did make it rather forgettable.

In the 19th Century, the Maritime Station was in fact a major player in the burgeoning cross-continental railway network. So much so, that the famous International Sleeping Car Company (Compagnie Internationale des Wagons Lits – CIWL) made Calais the starting-point for a good many of its international services, tapping into the healthy demand generated by wealthy Brits heading down from London and elsewhere. Those were, of course, the days when the (Simplon) *Orient Express* had through coaches from Calais as far as Istanbul and Athens (a service which managed to hold out until the early 1970s, having restarted in 1919), and when the *Indian Mail/Peninsular Express* would take you straight from Calais on a two-night journey to the Southern Italian port city of Brindisi, where you could board ships to Cairo and Mumbai.

Even though the range of direct destinations was reduced by the mid-1980s, it was still impressive, and yet again I have to acknowledge the lasting impression glancing up at the station departures board made on me. The table below shows a list of the direct destinations still accessible from Calais Maritime station at that time in the 1980s:

Austria	Innsbruck
France	Paris, Lille, Marseille, Nice, Quimper, Lourdes, Bordeaux, Hendaye, Annecy, Bourg St Maurice, St Gervais, Fréjus St Raphael, Tarbes, Avignon, Briançon, Toulouse, Brive, Narbonne, Cerbère, Strasbourg
Italy	Milan, Genoa, Ventimiglia (the Flandres-Riviera Express); Venice, Trieste, Rimini, Ancona, Rome (Italia Express); Albenga, San Remo, Bologna
Spain	Port Bou (the Flandres-Roussillon); Irun
Switzerland	Basle, Zürich, Chur, Interlaken, Chiasso, Bern, Brig

Again, the thought that you could get off the ferry and step onto a train heading straight to Venice or Rome seemed like an intoxicating mix of science fiction and *Wicker's World* glamour to me. Admittedly, I wasn't travelling quite so far on this particular occasion but that didn't matter – my next leg would see me heading to Paris for the first time in my life – could things be any more exciting? Today of course, London to Paris on Eurostar can be done in just over two hours direct. But back then, once arrived in Calais, it was still another three hours from the coast to the capital. Glancing out at the passing

French countryside really felt like a journey into the unknown, and my nerves increased as we approached Paris, where I knew I was going to have repeat the station to station kerfuffle of London – but for the first time in one of Europe's biggest cities. And I was also getting pretty tired by this point, much later on in the day. As so often in life, however, the prospect is generally far worse than the reality, and relying on my A Level French and the kindness of strangers, getting from the Gare du Nord to the Gare de Lyon on the metro didn't seem too massive a challenge in the end (the constant luggage lugging aside).

By the time I got to Paris Lyon station, it was gone 23.00. It was a very hot, balmy night too and the whole station seemed to glow somehow in a kind of hot orange light which made the contrast with a chilly grey Wolverhampton earlier that morning seem even greater. This is yet another of my abiding memories. I suppose it's partly to do with overcoming your fears and managing something you were apprehensive about; partly about doing something for the first time that at the time feels momentous; and partly about the complete contrast between where you start and finish, and all within a waking day. The last leg was imminent – find the train to Lyon and get on board.

As a major Paris terminus, the Gare de Lyon is a truly grand and imposing station, and I surprised myself in quickly managing to find the right platform. Even though the final stretch was an overnight journey of about six-and-a-half hours (around only two hours in today's high-speed world), I hadn't reserved a couchette, so made do with a seat in what looked like a quiet compartment. I remember saying 'bonsoir' to the solitary soldier sitting smoking in the dark by the window, all James Dean and Marlon Brando. He took one (disdainful) look at me (all Worzel Gummidge and Adrian Mole by that point) and just totally ignored me as I struggled getting my cases onto the luggage rack, sweating and panting like a 70s TV star called in for police questioning. I didn't care how uncool I was by then though; it was late and I was exhausted. When the train pulled out just after midnight, I think I fell asleep more or less instantly, and woke up shortly before we arrived in Lyon Perrache station at about 6.30 the following morning. I then had a few hours to look round the city and get some breakfast before getting a bus out into deepest Auvergne to start my next adventure working at a French school.

Walking around the city centre, I was instantly in awe of Lyon – it just seemed so different, so French, so glamorously sophisticated. I looked up at the Basilica of Notre Dame de Fourvière and couldn't believe it was only the previous morning that I'd set off from Wolverhampton. I followed signs for the Place des Terraux and crossed over one of the bridges onto the Presqu'Île – the very centre of the city, on a piece of land between the Rhone and the Saone, the two mighty rivers that flow through Lyon. Tucking into a croissant and coffee at a little cafe on the square that Monday morning, watching people starting their week, I can honestly say I've rarely since recaptured that same sense of achievement, contentment and adventure, despite it again being a relatively tame and local endeavour, in comparison with many of today's teenagers off backpacking in the jungles of the Far East and South America. And it was also a reasonably cheap undertaking - £37.20 for a single train ticket from Wolverhampton to Lyon! Those really were the days.

Train travel thoughts W

Don't be daunted by long journeys with multiple legs – it always works out in the end and leaves you with a great sense of achievement.

X

X – for eXotic – on the Red Lizard from Metlaoui to Redeyef

Route: Metlaoui – Seldja – Redeyef – Metlaoui

I've never knowingly been anywhere beginning with an X so have had to be a little creative again, but X for eXotic seems more than an apt description for this particular journey. This service was a popular tourist ride in Southern Tunisia, starting out from the small town of Metlaoui, about twenty-five miles south-west of the city of Gafsa. Even before you get on the train, it feels like an adventure – you're as good as on the way to the Sahara desert in the foothills of the Atlas Mountains. In the exotic stakes, this is already beating Settle to Carlisle for me, as wonderful as that route is. Add into the mix the North African sun, palm trees and camels, and you know this isn't the 8.55 from Birmingham New Street. I heard several people in the queue say the train and surrounding scenery had been used in the 1989 film, *Indiana Jones and the Last Crusade*. Doing the 45 km journey to Redeyef and back made that claim seem totally believable but I suspect it's one of those unfounded rumours that may have been put about by the tourist board back in the day.

At the time we did this journey, there were still several daily departures during the summer months, so the queue to join the small train wasn't horrendous. The train was made up of about six carriages that clearly had some age to them – vintage design, rustic wooden panels and old inscriptions in French and now Arabic. They'd actually been built in Belgium in the early 1900s and had the look of old Orient Express carriages such as I've seen on photos from the time. Before they ended up in North Africa (transporting the Bey of Tunis and his courtly entourage for many years), it is of course more than likely that several if not all the carriages had at some point been used in any number of grand old European express trains. In a strange way, I thought it was a little sad to think of a carriage that may once have transported royalty between Calais and Venice now shunting me (and Janice and Fred from Macclesfield) backwards and forwards on this sandy Saharan stretch. Is it an example of the mighty having fallen? But then again, is it sad? Looked at in another way, it's arguably a good thing that this old-timer was still in service and bringing pleasure to the travelling masses (about 100 passengers per ride), as well as providing a useful tourist income to a fairly remote and poor part of Tunisia. Trains, like all of us, I suppose, have lives that consist of different chapters. We adapt, reinvent ourselves and move with the times, if we're able to. Maybe it's just all about perspective.

Whatever the case, now beautifully restored after their previous lives and incarnations, the carriages oozed charm, and you could easily believe they once ran from Paris to Nice and beyond. They also really added to that sense of this being a very special journey. The windows were of the old-fashioned push-down into the side of the train type, which was more than welcome in the heat, and also meant unimpeded views on the way to the magnificent Seldja Gorge. I must admit this ride wasn't something I knew of before we went to Tunisia, but I'm so glad we found out about it while we were there and were able to make the trip, which is – outside of camels - probably the only way to visit the gorges of Seldja and the beautiful red and pink split rock canyons that surround them.

Describing the views as breathtaking is of course a little glib, but that's exactly what they were. We passed truly spectacular desert canyons (think *Indiana Jones* again), went through mountain tunnels, over steel bridges, glimpsed natural water springs and small, verdant oases. I looked around at my fellow tourists and you could tell that people were so overwhelmed, they just didn't know what to look at first. The train stopped a couple of times en route to allow us to get off and explore nearby. The photo opportunities were quite remarkable – the pink and cream rockscapes, the endless sandy vistas, the desert – it all felt so other-worldly, as I'm sure it did for the other assorted Northern Europeans who seemed to make up the majority of the train's passengers. And during these desert pauses, the train just stood there, quietly posing like an incredibly photogenic Hollywood star – 'le Lézard Rouge,' this faded yesteryear icon, still looking glamorous and loving the desert limelight. The two-hour round-trip was a real treat, and somehow all the more so for knowing that it was taking you somewhere so genuinely remote, different and beautiful.

Sadly, the dip in tourism after the Tunisian terror attacks saw the train slip back out of action for some time again and, as far as I can gather, it has since been further beset by problems, putting it well and truly out of operation for the foreseeable future. But if the history of this train and its carriages has taught us anything, it's that you should never write off a grand old dame – and I sincerely hope it's just enjoying some respite before it embarks on its next adventurous chapter.

Train travel thoughts X

It's often worth doing a bit of research to see if there are any narrow-gauge or tourist lines near where you're staying – they often make for an interesting outing.

Y

Y - For 'whY didn't I ever travel on this train?!' Paris to Lisbon on the Sud Express

Route: Paris Austerlitz – Bordeaux – Dax – Hendaye – Irun – Burgos – Salamanca – Pampilhosa – Coimbra - Lisbon

I know, I'm taking shameful alphabetical liberties now. But I wanted to include this train in the book as it's one of my all-time biggest railway regrets – somehow I just never got round to taking a trip on it, despite having intended to for years (the best laid plans and all that). So for me personally, it's a great shame and all the more so because it was such a classic long-distance train, with an equally long and illustrious history – a missed opportunity. Of course, it is still possible to get from Paris to Lisbon by rail but only with a fair few changes and overnight stays.

Though I never travelled on it, I did at least get to see it once. In 1992 I was enjoying a few days' break in Paris and found myself at the Gare d'Austerlitz one morning (as you do). Hearing the announcement of its imminent departure, and with time to spare to catch the local train I was waiting for, I headed over to the platform for a look-see. And there it was, sitting there waiting patiently for the off at 08.42, a glorious sight of assorted coach and carriage types. There were seating coaches going only as far as the Spanish border at Irun on Spain's Atlantic coast. In addition, there were sleeping and couchette cars heading all the way to Lisbon, along with others that would branch off en route for Porto, Portugal's second city in the north of the country (see P2). There were even carriages for a place I'd never heard of at that point, Vigo, a resort on Spain's far west Atlantic coast to the north of Portugal.

Looking up at the projected arrival times filled me with awe and envy – it was due to reach its various destinations around twenty-four hours later – a whole day for the lucky passengers to relax and watch the French, Spanish and Portuguese countryside go by. I decided there and then this was definitely a journey to add to my bucket list, but as mentioned, it was another casualty of never-getting-round-to-it syndrome. I presumed those passengers doing the full stretch had their own provisions on board, as I noticed there was no dining car - so it'd be self-catering all the way. By this point in time, this seemed to be the case for most international trains but it must have come as a bit of a shock for those finding out the hard way. Catering did apparently make something of an occasional comeback on the train years later but relying on the certainty of a dining car became an ever-increasing gamble.

At one point, a man with a cigarette leaning out of the window must have spotted me walking backwards and forwards on the platform and called out to ask me in accented French if I was looking for someone (I was actually looking to see if I could 'get hold' of a train sign). I replied that I was just admiring the train – he raised an eyebrow but agreed, the Sud Express was quite something. I asked him if he was going on holiday; it turned out he was going back home to Portugal to see his father who'd been taken ill. Somehow, this ended up turning into a lengthy conversation, and when the whistle finally blew to signal the off we were still nattering away. As the train suddenly jolted into motion, the smoking stranger leaned further out of the window and started waving, quite animatedly, as if we were old mates who'd known each other years. I was slightly taken aback at this; it just wasn't something I'd expected. I then found myself waving back at him, quite awkwardly and self-consciously – it must have looked like a clumsily reworked scene from *Brief Encounter* to anyone watching, not that they probably were, and not that it remotely mattered. It just seemed such an unanticipated small moment of intimacy. Who knows, in an alternative universe we could have ended up as good friends, meeting for a drink and a curry every few months. But in this one, our paths never crossed again of course, and sadly, it was also my last brief encounter with this famous train.

The Sud Express (South Express, Surexpreso in Spanish, Sud Expresso in Portuguese) had started life over a hundred years before in 1887. It was one of the great routes operated by the aforementioned CIWL, the brainchild of Belgian railway guru, Georges Nagelmackers. For the first years of its life, it was one of the many great trains that set out from Calais Maritime, travelling via Paris and Madrid to Lisbon and completing the journey in less than forty-eight hours. From 1890, Paris replaced Calais as the point of departure and remained so for the rest of its history. The importance of the connection with Lisbon wasn't just direct access to Portugal's capital city but the shipping routes that were available from Lisbon to Brazil and other parts of South America – so in this sense, the Sud Express was far more than 'just' an express train to the European south. The train's significance was further amplified a few years later with the inauguration of another of Nagelmackers' great train ideas, the Nord Express (North Express), which created a direct connection between Paris and Saint Petersburg. This now meant it was possible to travel all the way from northern Russia to southern Portugal (and beyond) with just one change of train in Paris. In a way, this wasn't quite true because of the gauge differences in Europe – it wasn't until the 1970s that passengers on the Sud Express didn't have to switch carriages at the French-Spanish border; from 1973 they could stay on the train now equipped with changeable bogies able to cope with the track variation.

Over the years, it ceased operation on a number of occasions for a variety of reasons. It was suspended for two years because of the Spanish Civil War in the late 1930s, and then again from 1940-45 because of the Second World War. It was also beset by a number of serious accidents, perhaps the most serious of which was a head-on collision with another train in Portugal on September 11th, 1985. Around 150 people were killed in the explosions caused by the crash, making it the country's worst ever rail disaster.

In 1989, it was ironically an improvement in French railway services that constituted its next challenge – the opening of the French 'LGV Atlantique' service that enabled speedier connections between Paris and the French south west. Though the direct through service from Paris survived for a few more years, it was eventually dropped to make way for more regular TGV services to the French-Spanish border at Hendaye/Irun. So by the mid-1990s, the Sud Express was truncated from Hendaye to Lisbon and back only, but still with second class seating accommodation, six-berth couchette coaches and first class sleeping compartments for one, two or three passengers.

Between the 1970s and 1990s, the train had been particularly popular with Portuguese 'guest workers' in France, Germany and the Benelux countries. All these countries had easy and regular connections to Paris, and the Sud Express was still a relatively cheap way of heading back home to see family – as it was for my *Brief Encounter* chum above. The advent of cheap flights, however, along with a hugely improving Portuguese economy (that saw fewer people wanting and needing to leave home for work) eventually saw a marked dip in the train's Portuguese patronage. Nonetheless, it still trundled along for years, despite more overtly negative mood music from around 2010, when the Portuguese government first proposed its withdrawal. Part of this negativity related to a growing Spanish and Portuguese disinclination towards night trains, which at that point was increasingly shared across the rest of Europe, as mentioned. The final nail in the coffin came with the outbreak of the Covid-19 pandemic in March 2020. It's been suggested in some quarters that the Portuguese and Spanish governments readily jumped on the pandemic as an excuse to axe the service, which may well be the case. It's certainly true that with its final withdrawal in 2020, another grand old European express disappeared from the timetables, and with it my (and others') last opportunity to travel on it.

As a footnote to this section, I'd like to dwell briefly on a few other French-Iberian trains that went the same way as the Sud Express, though in most cases much sooner. As noted, the change in gauge between France and Spain meant that the vast majority of international rail traffic stopped at the border – on the Atlantic side at the first station in Spain, Irun, and at Port Bou on the Mediterranean coast. There were a number of direct trains from Paris to both these small towns. Port Bou in particular received a large number of services from France and elsewhere in Europe, given its proximity to Barcelona and Valencia. Up until the 1980s, however, there were a few other trains with adjustable bogies that travelled beyond the border; the following table offers a list of some of these, along with a few other notable trains that journeyed down from elsewhere in Europe into Spain.

Train name	From	To
-	Paris Austerlitz	Irun/Madrid/Algeciras (for Gibraltar)
-	Stuttgart	Irun
-	Calais	Hendaye/Irun
Camino Azul	Amsterdam/Brussels/Paris	Port Bou
EC Catalan Talgo	Geneva	Barcelona
EC Pau Casals	Zürich/Milan	Barcelona
EN Joan Miro	Paris Austerlitz	Barcelona

Flandres Roussillon	Calais Maritime	Port Bou
Hispania (Express)	Copenhagen/Hamburg/ Dortmund	Port Bou
Hispania/ Mont Blanc	Basle/Geneva	Port Bou
Iberia Express	Paris Austerlitz	Irun
La Palombe Bleue	Paris Austerlitz	Madrid
La Puerta del Sol	Paris Austerlitz	Madrid
Mozart	Salzburg/Munich	Port Bou
Paris Cote Vermeille	Paris Austerlitz	Port Bou
Schwarz- wald Express	Hamburg/Geneva/Lyon	Port Bou
Valencia Express	Paris Austerlitz	Port Bou

Although the above is a list of 'those we have lost', the

good news is that the future is looking brighter. A new direct TGV was recently launched between Paris and Barcelona, for example, taking less than seven hours – a very comfortable morning into late afternoon journey. And one of the new railway kids on the block, the Dutch-Belgian company European Sleeper, is currently planning to launch a new seventeen hour service from Amsterdam and Brussels to Barcelona. If successful, this would be the first ever direct connection between Amsterdam and the Catalan capital. The same company launched a new direct sleeper service between Brussels/Amsterdam and Berlin/Prague last year, so the prospect looks very encouraging.

Train travel thoughts Y

If there's a particular train you'd really like to travel on, don't be a casualty of never-getting-round-to-it syndrome – swinging axes are quite often unpredictable.

Z

Z1 – Zürich to Villach – back on the EN Zürichsee (Lake Zürich)

Route: Zürich – Sargans – Buchs – Feldkirch – Innsbruck – Schwarzach St. Veit - Villach

This was another night train trip, this time from Switzerland to Austria – a nine hour journey of just over 600 km. The Zürichsee (see J – Jesenice to Zagreb) consisted of a mixture of day cars, couchette coaches and sleeping cars. I was heading for the city of Villach in the south-eastern Austrian state of Carinthia (Kärnten in German), near the Slovenian border. Other coaches were heading for Budapest via Vienna, while some were on their way to Belgrade via Slovenia and Croatia, so it took a few minutes to make sure I was getting into the right carriage.

As soon as I got on, I was pleasantly struck by how few people were travelling. Yet again, I'd taken the chance of booking into a six-berth couchette and was delighted to see just one other occupant: a man who'd already got into bed, and whose full conversational repertoire consisted of 'Guten Abend' – this suited me down to the ground. We were in a second-class Swiss carriage and I was impressed by the quality – a plump white pillow, spotless bedding, a clean compartment, plenty of room – this certainly wasn't slumming it. The train pulled out just after 21.30, right on time.

I'd enjoyed the few days I'd spent in Zürich. It's a handsome city (with another imposing station) but for me, the things that made it interesting were more to do with the surroundings. Admittedly, the medieval old town that straddles the Limmat River is very picturesque (and I also loved the city views from the huge Polyterasse at Zürich University) but the views of the mountains as seen from a boat ride on Lake Zürich were much more my sort of thing. By the time I got on the train to leave, I was very tired and ready for a good night's sleep. This was partly my own fault, having walked miles and miles as you often do when visiting a big city (Switzerland's largest) for the first time, but the previous night in the hotel had not been good. I'd booked a room in a 'cheap-ish' hotel near the station (I say cheap-ish – by Swiss standards; astronomical anywhere else) and realised when I got there why it was in a lower price category – basically, calling it a bit of a sh*t-hole would have been talking it up, but it was a decent enough room and had a loo and shower. Review complete. For a couple of nights it'd be fine. And the first night was in fact perfectly ok, but night two seemed to be turning into an episode of Brian Clemens' 1970s *Thriller* series.

I'd gone to bed fairly early, only to be disturbed by the room telephone ringing. When I got up to answer it, I could only hear breathing... and it wasn't mine. I put the receiver down and got back into bed thinking nothing further of it. An hour later, the same thing happened again. After the third time, I started to feel a bit unnerved so I rang reception. They said they hadn't put anyone through, so it must have been a call from another room in the hotel – not very reassuring. Unfortunately, things carried on like this for the rest of the night, getting even worse when at some point there was a slow series of knocks on the door. I didn't open it but stood right behind it and asked hesitantly (in my best macho German) who was there, clutching my chunky Alan Bennett (hardback) as the only thing that came to mind for a weapon (quite what Mr Bennett would make of his literary endeavours being considered for such potentially thuggish purposes, I don't know); no reply was forthcoming. After a while, I heard footsteps slowly moving away. I have to say this was one of the most unnerving nights I've ever had in a hotel, and I was relieved but exhausted when morning came. I never did get to find out what was going on – was there a crazed psychopath at large? Was it some perverted insomniac's idea of passing the time? Was it just drunken devilment? I'll never know.

So climbing into my bunk on the Zürichsee that night was a welcome bit of peace and quiet. I could hear my faceless fellow traveller snoring quietly already, and was following his example very shortly afterwards. I did wake up at one point to the terrible thought that he might have been the previous night's mystery knocker...but quickly put it out of my mind and reproached myself for watching too much rubbish on TV.

This particular train is one of several that still run today via a slightly amended route. Train services between Switzerland and Austria have always been good in terms of regularity and reliability. For years, the Franz Schubert, Transalpin and Zürichsee trundled backwards and forwards between Basle/Zürich and Vienna, with additional services to Innsbruck/Salzburg and Villach/Graz/Klagenfurt. The Arlberg Express once ran on the same route (Vienna to Zurich and Basle), heading on beyond the Swiss border up to Paris. This was the only train that ever ran from Vienna to Paris via Switzerland (all other routes favouring Germany) but it sadly no longer exists. These days the Transalpin is one of the few connections to still run under the same name but as an upgraded EC train. Most of the others operate under the Railjet brand.

In a way, I was being really foolish again – foolish in the sense that I was travelling through some of the world's most stunning scenery in the dead of night. The stretch between Zürich and Innsbruck is breathtaking, as the train travels briefly through Liechtenstein into Feldkirch, Austria (a little known town outside of Central Europe but beautiful and definitely worth a visit). It then moves into the rugged mountainous Arlberg region, before entering the Tyrol (again, just gorgeous). The onward route after Innsbruck (still gorgeous) gradually heads south via Schwarzach St Veit (did I mention it's gorgeous?) and towards Villach – well, you've guessed it. So as efficient a means as it was of getting me from A to B (or Z to V), it did mean I was being massively short-changed scenically. I've since covered these stretches separately on more recent daytime journeys, having learned my lesson, but it's definitely something to think about when planning your travels.

At around 6.30 the next morning, the train – or at least my particular carriage and a few others – was arriving in Villach. I was kicking myself yet again, realising this was obscenely early and I would have to kick my heels for quite a while until I could reasonably ask if there was a chance of an early check-in at the Bed and Breakfast I'd booked. Villach is a lovely town to be kicking your heels in for a while, it's more the time of day I was doing it that was the issue. Villach, like Feldkirch, is another Austrian town that's relatively little known to Brits, who, in the main, tend to favour the ski resorts or the larger cities on the tourist radar. It's long been a hugely popular summer and winter destination for Northern Europeans, the Germans and Dutch especially, and there's very good reason for this. Straddling the Drava River and situated very close to the Italian and Slovenian borders, the town is surrounded by magnificent Alpine views, probably best taken in from the St. Jakob's church on the main square. There are lots of smaller hiking and skiing resorts nearby, while the town's thermal baths are a huge draw for holidaymakers, as are the Faak and Ossiach lakes just a short distance away.

But at 6.30 that morning, the only things of interest to me were some hot coffee and breakfast in the station cafe. I ended up ordering a bratwurst – it seemed a good idea at the time. As I bit into it, it spat hot fat back in my face as if I'd offended it. I persevered but it still won the day by saddling me with severe indigestion that I'm not sure I've ever fully recovered from. After this undignified trial by sausage, the time had at least moved on and I decided it was worth taking a chance on the B & B letting me check in a bit earlier. Luck was on my side, and I was soon sprawled out on an Austrian feather bed, getting a couple of extra hours' sleep to set me up for the rest of the day looking round the town and its sights. Subdued burp – excuse me.

Z2 – Zakopane to Krakow – on a Polish regional train

Route: Zakopane – Nowy Targ – Chabowka – Sucha Beskidzka – Krakow

I must admit I'd never heard of Zakopane until my friend Marek told me it was a must-see in any Polish tour. And if anyone would know, it would be him. His job with Polish Railways (PKP) took him not only all over Poland by train, but over the entirety of our amazing European railway network – there wasn't a single route, train service, town or air brake system he didn't know about; and couldn't talk about at great length. While I was often very interested to hear about the towns and trains, I sometimes had to cut him short on the intricacies of straight air applications and triple valve pressures... But as far as Zakopane was concerned, his recommendation was absolutely spot on.

The town itself is a charmingly rustic place with lots of wooden houses, souvenir shops and restaurants but it's not actually the main attraction – that honour goes to the amazing scenery that surrounds it. Zakopane in Poland's far south is the entry point into the Tatra Mountains, the highest mountain range in the country and also the Western Carpathians, for that matter. Marek and Beata (his wife) insisted we go up to Kasprowy Wierch, one of the highest and most popular peaks. I was relieved we could go up by cable car, so off we went to the cable car station. Nowadays, most people book advance tickets online but this was the 1990s... and so we joined the queue.

To say it was a long queue is like saying Hitler had a bit of a naughty streak. We waited and waited (for over three hours in the baking summer sunshine) until we finally got through and into the cable car. A bit of a trial but absolutely worth it – the views of the surrounding mountains were beyond stunning. Walking around up on the peak was completely overwhelming; the total thrill and beauty of this mighty natural landscape spanning the

Polish-Slovak border actually brought tears to my eyes, it was genuinely breathtaking. One thing that surprised me, given the massive number of people heading up there, was how quickly they seemed to disperse. I'd half expected it to be a bit like the typical church tower visit where you have to jostle with every other visitor for a view, but far from it. Being able to get away from the hordes up there really added to the feeling of peace that was as close to a spiritual experience as I think I've ever had. The light summer cloud drifting around further added to this ethereal feeling, it really was quite special. Coming back down to earth, I was also surprised to see national border posts dotted around so high up, and felt obliged to go for the compulsory tourist photo, standing with one foot in Poland, one in Slovakia.

After a delightful few hours hiking up there, it was time to offset any health and wellness benefits by indulging in a Polish picnic/cholesterol fest – sausage and salami, bread and beer, vodka and cheese. Oh yes, and more sausage. And beer. It was a good job we didn't have to go back down on foot. Once out of the cable car, we made our way to the railway station in the village to catch the next local train to Krakow, about 150 km to the north. It seemed like the perfect end to a summer's afternoon after a day of fresh mountain air, imposingly rugged scenery and culinary indulgence in the great outdoors. The train was waiting when we got to the station, so we jumped on and found some seats where the three of us could sit together. And no sooner had we sat down than the train pulled out, the late afternoon sunshine on our faces adding to the mellow vibe.

Even though Krakow really isn't that far away, the local train we were on took over four hours. Why would it take so long, you might ask – slow-going, mountainous terrain? Not really. Farm animals on the line? No. Engine trouble at Chabowka? No. Forty plus station stops? Yes. It really was remarkable that there could be so many scheduled stops en route. What was even more surprising was my reaction to this. Ordinarily, I'd be tearing my hair out or at least fidgeting like a five-year-old with fleas after an hour of this. But it had been such a genuinely chilled day, and the wonderful combination of fresh air, sunshine, company and alcohol had got me to a rare place where each stop somehow managed to wind me down rather than up, a bit like the hypnotist counting down. It was like taking part in a strange, meditative ritual – a sort of railway equivalent of the stations of the cross – even if the stations all had names which made me think of the lines of letters you have to read out when having an eye-test. The hypnotic rattle of the train added to this effect and consolidated the semi-spiritual quality of the day.

By the time we reached Krakow's main station, the evening sun was beginning to set, and we walked back to the apartment Marek had organised for us. It's sad that as life moved on, we eventually lost touch, as occasionally happens with friends who live in different countries. And as also sometimes happens, we find ourselves thinking about them at some point for no particular reason. This prompted me to Google him to see if I could find a current email address or any other contact details. I was shocked instead to come across his obituary – he'd died in a swimming accident off the French coast near Bordeaux a couple of years earlier. I'd always assumed it'd be the fags and vodka that would get him in the end – he was pretty much a chain smoker. In fact, he was the only person I'd ever seen smoking in the shower; he'd once left the bathroom door open and I saw his arm stretching out from behind the shower curtain, lit cigarette in hand, and head repeatedly bobbing out for a swift drag.

Hearing of a friend's death is always a shock, even when – or perhaps especially when - it's someone we haven't been in touch with for some time. There is of course a lesson in this somewhere, no doubt something about not losing touch with people and not assuming it'll always be possible to pick up the thread again some time. But human nature being what it is, we're often defeated by our best intentions. Marek's death has inevitably made my memories of that day in Zakopane and the slow train back to Krakow all the more poignant. I hope he's still up there somewhere, swigging vodka on some celestial railway; and to vodka drinkers and train travellers everywhere – na zdrowie!

Train travel thoughts Z

Make sure to check the coach destination sign so you know you're in the right carriage – long distance trains often split off in several directions en route.

Always consider the pros and cons of night vs. day travel on your chosen route.

Choose station snacks with a degree of caution or: "ask yourself a question; do you feel lucky, punk?"

It's never a bad idea to send an old friend a postcard from your train travels – you never know, it might just rekindle a friendship.

Thank you for buying my book! I hope you enjoyed reading it. If you did, I'd be really grateful if you could leave a rating or short review (just a couple of words would be much appreciated) on Amazon – thank you.

INTERRAIL RAMBLINGS